MW00769785

Table of Contents

***

Along Came Zita ….

i

For Alaina & Olivia ....

Preface

***

So... let me start right off the bat by saying that, yes, I do believe in ghosts, or to be more precise, that I am certain there is unexpected spiritual activity all around us. This is something which I can honestly say that I have been aware of for most of my life. *And that's a good thing,* or this entire record of what occurred between me, and Zita would not make much sense to me, or to anyone else for that matter. Zita Johann wanted to make sure I understood why she still comes to me at the most interesting times. I hear her voice as clear as day:

Get my word out there and let people know what happened with my work ... and don't stop until you are satisfied with how you tell it.

So now ... after many years of procrastination, with plenty of starts and stops along the way, I think I've gotten it down pretty well. Zita would be fascinated with how things have turned out; of that I am certain. With this book of mine, she would finally feel hopeful that her book and screenplay entitled "After the End" would be credited back to its rightful creator. And then maybe, we both can finally get some rest!

This is my true story about how it all began, then ended, and now begins again, *after the end.*

***

Chapter One

Up the River

***

What do you want to be when you grow up? That age-old question is asked of children numerous times during childhood, and it certainly was asked of me. Mothers and fathers want to know what greatness their children are destined for, aunts and uncles are curious about what makes a particular child tick, and even classmates and teachers make it a common topic in classrooms and on playgrounds. Answers always vary from child to child, but inevitably they will include such

1

careers as doctor, fireman, teacher, athlete, or astronaut. In my younger years, I likely answered that question in similar ways. I didn't have the confidence then to stand out from the crowd, but all that time I did know in my heart that I just wasn't really into whatever expected career answer I would toss out.

Some years later, though, at the lofty age of seventeen, and after much thought but very little planning, I reached a decision about my future. It would be an answer to the question that was a good bit different from what might be considered a traditional career goal, but one that would give my life passion and purpose. It was this decision, along with its pursuit, which led me to experience the gift of *Zita.*

As far back as I can remember, I was fascinated by what I saw on television. My favorite spot was in the middle of the room.

I spent many hours sitting cross-legged on the carpeted floor in front of that colorful *wonderland-in-a-box* absolutely engrossed in, and completely enthralled by, my nightly escape. Every night I watched singers, actors, and dancers perform, and all the while, whether I knew it or not, I was configuring how I might one day be a part of this dreamy kingdom.

As a teenager in the 1970's, the entertainers who performed in my living room each night were incredibly talented. Icons like Dean Martin, Lucille Ball, and Sonny and Cher made each night glorious fun. I drank in every detail of each performance. They all had a zeal which radiated directly at me, as if I was their most prized fan, and I desperately wanted a piece of it. I watched Donny and Marie Osmond with particular eagerness, and Marie's great charm and bubbly personality, together with her beautiful brown eyes and warm smile, was a potent combination. So much so, that I will freely admit she was my first-ever celebrity crush!

However, John Travolta was a very popular actor of my day in the hit show *Welcome Back Kotter,* and he truly captured my attention. Yes, *up your nose with a rubber hose* resonated within me. The more I watched him, the more I knew that I had to be on a television show just like he was.

Actually, my first taste of being involved in a production was in 1970, when I was nine years old. That was when I had first experienced the lure of a live production. Tappan Zee Elementary School was performing *"The Mikado,"* and at the time, I had no idea what a drama club was or that one even existed. But I did know that I wanted to get involved, even though it was long after the time for auditions and the subsequent weeks of rehearsals. I had mentioned my interest to one of the teachers, and she didn't hesitate to put me to work on opening night, greeting parents and family members at the door and handing out programs. I felt that my job was an important one, it was fun being "in charge" of something, and I was soon hooked. I plastered a smile on my face and offered everyone a warm welcome. When the room was filled and there were no more programs to pass, my job was over. There was a quiet buzz throughout the room; energy was building for the start of the play.

I had a reserved seat on the front row for the performance, and not long after I took my seat, the lights dimmed. The crowd hushed instantly, and then the massive velvet curtains drifted apart. I sat up straight in my chair, and I do not think I moved a muscle for the next hour. I remember being astonished by the set changes on stage, the costumes, the lighting, the makeup, and most of all, *the acting.* As I sat there in glorious wonder, it occurred to me that there were so many things needing to come together on this one night. I recognized that the roles which everyone played were important to the overall success of the performance, and I began thinking about how essential it was to the performance that the prominent roles be taken by those who knew what had to be done. I was consumed with the idea of having such a responsibility, and I sat mesmerized throughout the entire play. That night, when I was home in bed with my head resting on my pillow, I played scenes from the performance over and over in my head, pondering how they could have been performed better. As I did so, *I was always one of the lead actors.*

Though I had a vivid imagination as a child, my family itself had deep roots within a firm reality, more or less. My mom, Rita as she was called, was an amazing mother. She was kind and understanding, but she was also a no-nonsense kind of woman. She was second-generation from a large Italian family. Along with her, my dad, three sisters, lone brother and I all lived with my grandmother in a large, *center hall Colonial home* in the hamlet called Sparkill, New York. The center hall Colonial is a style of homes which had originated when early colonists arrived in North America, since it could be built quickly in order to protect settlers from the elements. It became popular in the area thereafter since it was spacious, comfortable, and rather handsome.

There were, and still are, quite a few celebrities who have homes within and around the hamlet of Sparkill, as well as in the nearby riverfront Village of Nyack. It was a fifteen-minute bus ride from Sparkill to Nyack, a route that travels through two other riverfront communities, Piermont and Grandview. As time progressed, Nyack became very culturally diverse, leading to its modern-day incarnation as a small city on the Hudson River laden with art dealers, boutiques, and coffee shops. Antique shoppers bustle about the town on any given weekday, with the number multiplying greatly on weekends. During my childhood, my dad was a hard-working man who was dependable, and who expected that his children would find success within typical fields of work as they became adults. My town was quiet, and people respected one another for the most part. Sparkill, itself, was located eighteen miles north of New York City and one mile inland from the majestic Hudson River. Back then, the town had a relaxed suburban feel bordering on farmland, with several horse stables and unique, family-owned businesses, restaurants, and shops.

Quite possibly, some of my propensity for acting came to me naturally from my mother. Seeing her in action would lead one to wonder how she eluded talent scouts in her younger years. She and her older sister, Vera, had a natural and effective comedic timing, and when they were together, it was always a recipe for near calamities and hysterical shenanigans. I remember one afternoon when they had gone shopping together in nearby Paramus, New Jersey. They traveled the backroads of Northern Bergen County, New Jersey, to get there. This particular spree would last until early evening, and on their way home, they somehow became lost. In an attempt to get turned around and back on familiar roads, Mom made a U-turn on a side street and unceremoniously backed her car into a large tree as she was attempting to complete the maneuver.

When they got home, they found Dad and Grandma waiting anxiously on our driveway, and Mom had prepared, immediately launching into her story.

"Well, I realized we were going the wrong way, so I backed up, hit a tree, and then *got the hell out of there.* At least, the tree was still standing as I drove away," she said in her off-handed but hilarious way. This left my dad and grandma shaking their heads, and thankfully, hitting the tree had not caused any major damage to the car, just a few scratches.

I think that it was quite realistic to believe that, in the back of her mind, my mom always knew that I was headed in the direction of doing something creative with my life, owing to the fact that I had shown great interest in many of the arts beginning at a very early age. Mom worked very hard at a local grocery store, and during the course of her work, she became friendly with the famous actor Jon Voight, who was one of her regular customers. Every time he came into the store, my mom would engage in conversation with him, which she could not wait to tell us all about later that same night. During one of her conversations with Mr. Voight, she even went so far as to mention to him that I might become an actor one day, and she was thrilled to tell me that evening that he had wished me luck, laughing all the while as she told me. I believe at that time, she had said this more as a conversation item, not because she truly believed it would be so.

So, little did she know how prophetic her comment would turn out to be. I finally spotted Mr. Voight myself one day while ice skating on the local pond between Sparkill and Piermont. He had his son and daughter with him, and though I had seen *Deliverance,* it still took me a minute or two to realize he was the actor my mom had been telling us about for months. Though I wanted so badly to do so, at the time, I didn't have the courage to introduce myself to him. That opportunity did come back to me later in my life; however, when I ran into him again at the first *Turner Classic Movie Festival*. This time, I did introduce myself, and was more than gratified when he smiled in recognition that I was the son my mom had mentioned to him all those years before, back at the grocery store.

However, before that momentous occasion would take place, there was a sort of uneven path getting there. During my latter teen years, my travels to and from Sparkill and Nyack gave me plenty of time to daydream about being on television or on stage and becoming as famous as the celebrities who lived nearby. I would go into Nyack with friends to shop, or have ice cream and coffee, or just to wander its streets window shopping by myself. And so, when the proverbial lightbulb came on for me almost eight years after that first night as host for the theatrical production at Tappan Zee Elementary, it was with complete confidence that I began to see my life as a successful actor. Initially, I envisioned myself on a television show, just like my idol John Travolta. With unshakeable finality, I imagined myself becoming an idol of teens everywhere, teens who impatiently waited each week for the one night that my own show would be broadcast into their living room.

As to my reasoning? Well, for instance, I knew I had the same kind of charm that Travolta had: my energy matched his energy, my talent mirrored his talent. *What more did I need?* The truth was: *I had absolutely no idea how anyone - an actor, a dancer, or a singer - made their way into show business.* But that didn't deter me. I was sure that I would find a way, because deep inside I knew with absolute certainty that this was who I was meant to be.

Despite my great sense of self-confidence, I can't say that my decision provided my mother with any of the same exuberance when I decided to make my proclamation official. It was in 1978, when I was seventeen, that I decided to share my career decision with my mother. I didn't know what kind of reaction I would get, but up until the moment I disclosed my dreams, it never crossed my mind that it would be at all controversial. *To me, it was a no-brainer.* Not only was I convinced that I was choosing the right career for me, but I also firmly believed that the career had chosen me, as well. That was how confident I felt, and at this point, I was sure that life as an actor was meant for me.

I had spent this particular evening reading about John Travolta and his daily schedule in Hollywood and doing so had only served to fuel my burgeoning plan. *Why wait to fulfill my destiny?* So with the utmost conviction, I approached my mom while she was in the kitchen after dinner. "Mom, I'm going to drop out of high school and get a job on a show like John Travolta."

"Oh, nooooo you're not." Her response was instant and firm. She had not even looked up from the table.

"Yes, I am," I said adamantly, my voice holding steady. I then held out the article about Travolta. "Look, this article says that he has been taking his high school classes between his work shifts on *Kotter* at the studio." I shrugged my shoulders, suggesting that I had everything all worked out.

"You are NOT quitting school, and that is that!" Her loud voice echoed around and bounced off of the kitchen walls, and she carried on putting away dishes and silverware as if her response had already put an end to my ridiculous assertion.

"But why not? If John Travolta can do it, why can't I?" My voice gave no hint of reconsidering my position. To me, I had just presented a rather clear and convincing argument, *an end-all,* as to why my plan was a solid one. I was certain that my mom could see the wisdom of my decision as clear as day.

Without any hesitation my mom answered emphatically, *"For starters, because you're no John Travolta!"*

I had no comeback for that particular statement, and so I decided to just let the discussion end for the moment. *There was always tomorrow!*

An hour later, up in my bedroom, it occurred to me that she was probably thinking, *"What the heck is up with this kid?"* I second-guessed myself for just a moment, not exactly sure what had gotten into me. Just as quickly, I realized I had no intention of changing my mind. Even if she was right, *and I was not John Travolta,* I knew that I could not allow that simple fact to stop me. *No* - I wasn't about to let such a little thing interfere with following my dream.

My mom must have sensed the depth of my determination, however, because she was worried enough to seek outside help. The appointment was made for the very next day! She insisted that I see the school psychologist to explain why I wanted to drop out of school, having convinced my principal that mine was an emergency case. *Seriously? For this I had to see the school psychologist?*

The psychologist's office was located in a small room off of the nurse's office where the daily, *I don't feel good, I'm going to throw up kids* would try to finagle a day off. When I got to the nurse's office that day, no one was there - no nurse and no waiting students. I stopped briefly and took a deep breath, and then I walked confidently right on back to see the psychologist. I knocked firmly on the open door, and his head, previously buried in a large textbook, lifted until our eyes met. He stood from behind his desk, waved me in, and then motioned for me to close the door behind me. He asked me to take a seat across from his desk, and without any welcoming chit chat, began the inquisition.

"So, Thomas, why do you want to leave school?" His voice was warm enough but seemed to lack much conviction. I had the feeling that he really wasn't too interested in changing my mind. *This shouldn't be too hard, I thought to myself.*

"I want to be an actor." I looked him straight in the eye and spoke calmly but forcefully.

"All right," he said. "I want to show you these cards and then you tell me what you see on them."

Inside, I laughed to myself. *You've got to be kidding me. Ink blots? Really?*

Before I could think of a smart-ass reply to the first card he held up, the door swung open and a girl who was a dead ringer for the folk singer Carly Simon way back in the 70's waltzed in and sat herself comfortably right on top of the psychologist's desk, directly in front of him. Her dark hair had streaks of blonde and hung carelessly down her back, and her eyes were wide, brown, and brimming with electricity. I could not believe it when she yanked up her long peasant-style skirt to show off her legs as she crossed one over the other. She leaned into the good doctor's face and asked in a sultry and raspy voice, *"How ya doing today, Doc?"*

The psychologist was clearly flustered. His face quickly grew red, and he bit his lip. He gestured nervously, arms waving about, trying unsuccessfully to get her off of his desk. "You cannot be in here. Come on now, *get off the desk,* you have to leave." I tried to keep my face from showing the amusement I was feeling, but I had a good idea I was failing at that.

"But why," she crooned," what are you guys talking about?" The girl made no move to get down from the desk. In fact, she turned to look at me and gave me a steamy smile and a conspiratorial wink. I could feel the blush making its way up my cheeks, and I am sure that the look on my face was worth more than a million bucks! I could not believe what I was seeing; it was right out of some Woody Allen script where Diane Keaton would go into some powerful and obscure, almost absurd, tirade meant to embarrass whatever man she had targeted for such exposure... *for whatever the reason.*

The psychologist started to make more of an effort to get her off his desk and out of the office. He stood up and alternately approached her and then backed away, all the while repeating his demand that she leave. She resisted playfully, relishing in his extreme discomfort, but eventually, the doc was able to evict her gently and firmly. She glanced back at me again before she left, and I lifted my chin in a friendly nod. The psychologist closed the door behind her, straightened his tie, and stammered, "Okay. Let's, um, yes, okay, so where were we?" He avoided making eye contact with me, and instead focused on the top of his desk. He shuffled a few papers, obviously lacking any organizational prowess, and then he tried to gather the jumbled inkblot cards. Soon frustrated with his inability to resume a normal meeting, he glanced in my direction. "Yes, uh, okay, never mind, you're fine. You can go. *We are done here.*"

I felt buoyed by having won that round so easily.
Next stop, Hollywood!

I strolled confidently into the living room after
school, and I told everyone that the psychologist had said
I was "fine." Surely, that would be enough to convince
my family that, indeed, it made sense for me to quit
school and immediately embark on my new career as an
actor. My dad shook his head in disbelief, but didn't
voice his opinion, which showed me how little stock he
put in what he thought was my *wild and worthless idea.*
He simply rattled his newspaper and returned his gaze to
the sports section. Since I had been so eager to win him
over, I mistook his silence to mean that he approved of
my decision. One of my sisters muttered a noncommittal,
"Cool," and I was left thinking *just wait and see* ....

My mom, however, was still not sold; and her
next move was to call Aunt Mary. Unlike my Aunt Vera,

my Aunt Mary Bianchi was actually in the entertainment business, and had become a popular public figure in Rockland County. She hosted a local cable show in 1973 called "The Mary Bee Show," which aired once a week. Right before dinner, I heard Mom on the phone, barely pausing to take a breath. Mom gave Aunt Mary the lowdown on my recent announcement and asked her for some advice. I couldn't hear what Aunt Mary was saying, but my mom nodded her head vehemently in agreement. I didn't have to wait long to hear the other side of the discussion. At dinner, Mom came loaded with Aunt Mary's wisdom.

"I spoke to Aunt Mary today," she said. "I told her that you still want to be an actor, and I asked her what you should do." Her face was set with the determined look of victory.

"Well, what did she say?" I doubted the advice would be something I wanted to hear, but I played along. After all, Aunt Mary was kind of a celebrity, and there was a remote possibility that she could steer me in the right direction.

With all the force she could muster, Mom stated, "She said you should forget about it, and I think she is right."

Okay, like that is going to work. NOT. "No matter what Aunt Mary thinks," I said, then I felt myself channeling Vinnie Barbarino's charisma, assertiveness, and *devil-may-care* attitude. "I am still going to be an actor." With that, I pushed back my chair as I stood upright, and then I sauntered out of the dining room doing a Brooklyn waltz.

So much for Aunt Mary's assistance in my burgeoning career. Arriving in my bedroom, I closed the door behind me and threw myself on my bed. *Alright, so maybe I wouldn't quit school just yet, but I was still going to be the next John Travolta. I was sure of that.*

Undaunted, the next day Mom had secured even more advice from Aunt Mary. It was clear that she wasn't going to just accept my decision. "Aunt Mary also said that you should join the drama club in school or go to the community playhouse to test your talent and see if you really have what it takes."

I am sure Mom hoped that suggestion would lead to showing me the error in my judgment about my own talent, *but I saw it differently.*

This time, Aunt Mary's advice actually gave me a reason to pause. Finding, and then actually joining, a like-minded group of thespians was something I had not yet considered myself, but it did seem to be a reasonable steppingstone. It might just hold the key to proving to my mom, and to everyone else for that matter, that I truly

had what it takes to be an actor.

With that in mind, the wheels in my mind began

accelerating.

No doubt, I was definitely on my way to becoming

a wildly successful actor....

***

Chapter Two

The Playhouse

***

I spent a good deal of time that night thinking about Aunt Mary's suggestion. I quickly dismissed the idea of joining a school drama group because I was sure that those students were no more knowledgeable than I was. Besides, I wanted to be done with school and my peers - *I was ready to go out and make my way as a critically-acclaimed actor on tv, in film, and on stage.*

However, it could be that Aunt Mary was on the right path suggesting that I join a professional group.

Getting involved with experienced, serious actors could help send me on my way toward achieving my dream, and I thought about all of the contacts I could make. I closed my eyes and pictured myself standing on stage with seasoned actors. If I truly wanted to learn, surrounding myself with those who had been acting much longer than I had been could only give me ideas and lessons to improve my craft. Instinctively, I knew that I could learn a lot from watching and listening. And any feedback I might get, though not easy to hear, would help propel me forwards. *If I'm going to open myself up to criticism, I'm going to get it from experienced thespians. A one-two punch from them will be much easier to take than from classmates known for spitting milk out of their noses.*

The following day, I researched community playhouses and made a few phone calls. I wanted to find a place that had frequent performances and also which had been in operation for a long time and so had established itself as a mainstay. After weighing my options, I settled on the Elmwood Playhouse in Nyack. It seemed to be one of the most active of the local theaters, and its location sold me on it. The Elmwood Playhouse held meetings on the first Monday of every month, and so I didn't have long to wait until I could check them out in person.

It was with excitement, but also a bit of nervous energy, that I headed to their next scheduled meeting. I took a deep breath, opened the door to the theater. I was feeling a little overwhelmed by all the adults chatting among themselves, and I felt absolutely alone for several minutes, but then soon someone stepped on stage and the noise in the room quieted down.

Walter was a tall and thin man in his thirties with a full beard and a loosely fitting red and tan flannel shirt draped over his Wrangler jeans. He introduced himself and welcomed all new members to the meeting. The format for the meeting seemed pretty standard: we would read from prepared minutes and make announcements about upcoming events. There were a few questions from audience members clarifying some of the announcements, but overall, the business portion of the meetings would never take too long. From my phone call with one of the members the week before, I knew that there would also be a performance of sorts that night, directed by a group member, which also sometimes had the intent of introducing up and coming talent.

Sure enough, a small group of members took the stage and performed a short piece which I had never seen before. It was some dramatic and romantic love story taking place between five young adults at a malt shop. Some of the actors seemed great. Everyone was attentive and encouraging, and I slowly began to feel at one with this group. In a way, you might say that I was feeling that I was *right at home*.

When the meeting was coming to a close for the night, everyone stood up and mingled about on stage and I realized how quickly the time had passed. Even though I was still a little shy, I knew that this was something I must learn how to do, and so I pushed myself beyond my comfort zone in order to meet some of the members. I began introducing myself, and then suddenly, a sparky, red-headed woman named Selma approached me and *introduced herself to me.* She had been involved in directing the Elmwood Players for several years, and she told me that she was always interested in helping new members to settle into the playhouse. Selma's energy was contagious, and I found it was easy for me to talk with her. After I told her a little about myself and my dreams of becoming an actor, she surprised me by saying, "Would you be interested in doing a few scenes by Jules Feiffer at the next meeting?"

"Sure!" I answered. *I had no idea who Jules Feiffer was. What had I gotten myself into? But I was intent on going full-speed ahead.* I was so excited that an actual director had taken an interest in me and had asked me to perform. *Maybe she had known John Travolta before he had gotten his big break! Let's go!*

From my perspective now as an adult, I can say wholeheartedly, I believe that to understand the desire to be an actor, you have to experience the stage. There is nothing like it in the entire world. A thousand eyes are watching each minute gesture, a thousand ears are hearing each little inflection of tone used to express words, all at the same time. *Everything matters!* It is all live and there are no extra takes, no edits, and no second chances! Of course, the experience of acting on stage is a trial by fire: *you either have it or you don't.*

I felt pretty confident that I had what it took even if I did, at the same time, recognize that up until that point in time I had little actual experience. Yet, I was not about to let that hold me back. With the script by Jules Feiffer given to me by Selma at the end of my first meeting, I rehearsed in my bedroom four times per day, every day, trying to use different voices and various speeds and tones for delivery. At the next meeting, I was fully committed to taking my first step towards proving my worth and talent as an actor.

Miss Selma directed her chosen group of actors, and we rehearsed our short scenes by Jules Feiffer before our scheduled performance time. Mr. Feiffer had won a

Pulitzer Prize for his work as an editorial cartoonist, and also an Academy Award for an animated, short film. I would learn later on that his body of work is endless and quite impressive, and looking back on it, at the time, I am glad that I did not have the foresight to do research on him or I would have felt more pressure to get everything just so. I was cast as an innocent love interest, *and I had one single line.* My job was to enter the stage, speak my one line to a fluttering ballerina who deems me unworthy of her love, who then flitters away, and then I was to exit stage left. That seemed easy enough to me.

"By the way, the house is packed tonight," Selma told us at the end of our last rehearsal. She smiled at me, then turned around to head down the wing, saying, as she walked away, *"Break a leg, everyone!"*

To this day, I am still unsure how I feel about that expression. *Where the hell did it come from?* It invokes within me everything about my fears, but also about my pride to do the profession of acting justice, *each and every time I walk out on stage.*

"You'll do fine," the ballerina said to me, catching me by surprise and off guard as I watched Selma take one of the other actors aside to have a few words with him. I realized that my anxiety must have been showing on my face, and so I immediately gave her a huge grin meant to charm her and show her that I was on top of my game.

"As will you!" I said to her, as if the act of sharing with her my positive energy would somehow enhance our performances.

I went to join the meeting before our scene would take place, and I wondered how natural it would feel to walk out on stage for the first time. *I felt a sense of urgency - I wanted to just get my part done and my line*

uttered correctly.

The time had come. I was backstage, ready,

willing, and able. I tried keeping my nerves as much

under control as possible. I peeked out at the auditorium

from offstage on the right wing, and the audience seemed

to be quite engrossed and engaged with the scene

unfolding before them. *That's a good sign!* Of course, for

these scenes, there were no special costumes, wardrobe,

or makeup, just our regular clothes and ordinary

appearance. For a moment, I wondered if I should have

dressed more formally and not in my jeans, sneakers, and

white button-down dress shirt. *Oh well, too late now!*

Before I knew it, I heard my cue. I took a deep breath

and put myself into the character I believed best fit the

scene – a noble romantic who had to deal with

unrequited love.

I waltzed confidently out on stage, right towards the ballerina. With a grand show of my presence, my arms outstretched, and putting my mind on just how Travolta would handle this line, I looked into her eyes and uttered the words just as I had rehearsed. They rolled off my tongue and there, it was done. I had delivered my one line and I had performed it to a packed house.

When I had walked out on stage that night, I did not really understand the meaning or the context behind the line. *"Stifled love makes me uncertain; you are bound to find somebody else."* My voice rang out loudly and clearly; however, *the audience immediately broke out in laughter.* This worried me a tremendous amount as I exited the stage. This was not the response I had expected. I was pretty sure I had performed it just as Selma had directed me. *What did I say or do wrong here? Why was it so funny?*

After the performance was over, I was a little nervous about what Miss Selma might have to say to me. As she made her way toward me, my stomach flipped and flopped. I wanted to hide for a second, but I also wanted some honest feedback. To my surprise, Miss Selma patted me on the back and said, "Congratulations, Tom. You did a great job!"

I smiled thinly and hesitated, but finally, I had to ask. "But why did the audience laugh?" I asked her.

Miss Selma's eyebrows lifted in surprise. "Tom, your line was supposed to be funny," she said. My stomach settled down, and I took the first normal breath I'd had since exiting the stage. I realized then that my hyperfocus on getting my line delivered correctly had made me miss the humorous context! *Lesson learned. I can be funny! I can deliver, and I am liking this! For sure, I want more.* I headed home that night with a huge grin on my face.

In hindsight, I know I should never begin a role by not doing my research, but luckily for me, my ignorance about Jules Feiffer that night had paid off that one time. By taking my line seriously, it had worked to increase the comical effect it had on the audience. *Who knows what would have happened if I had tried to say my line looking for laughs?* When my head hit the pillow later, I knew that my decision to pursue an acting career was now solidified, and the truth is, I have never forgotten my first line.

The next morning, I told my mom that I did okay. I wanted to give nothing away to her or to any of my family at this time. In fact, I played it like I was not certain this acting thing was for me. That would be the easiest way to keep them off of my back for now.

Soon after, Selma invited me to join a troupe of actors to study improvisation and burlesque techniques. I quickly agreed, again with no questions asked. *Should I be learning a lesson about not asking questions?* The troupe met every two weeks in the recreation room of a local church. We prepared scenes, tightened our improv skills, and performed at various social gatherings in the New York tri-state area. I was by far the youngest member of the group which may explain why I was unaware of the emphasis on the "social" part of these gatherings. Totally engrossed in learning the craft of improvisation, I didn't stop to notice that the shows served another purpose as well. The name of the troupe was "Singles on Stage" or "SOS," but even that didn't tip me off.

It was several weeks into my time with them that I finally started to realize that a major part of each performance was the social interaction between the cast and audience after each show. At one performance, there was a sign at the lobby door welcoming all to *singles night out. Okay, so maybe it did take a piano falling on my head for me to realize that more than acting was on the docket.*

I had been teamed up with a very funny woman for many of my scenes, and we hit it off right away. One night after we had finished our performance, she finally cornered me backstage. She had no idea that I had not picked up on the dual agenda for SOS, but her sincere talk with me that night helped clue me into the flirtatious happenings all around me at these gatherings. "So, Tom," she said," I think we are getting along pretty good here, but I think since I'm a little older, you're more of a fit for my daughter than me."

What?

She looked straight into my eyes, determined to let me down ever so gently, and I almost burst out laughing because that was when, with absolute certainty, it had finally dawned on me what was going on with SOS. *How could I have been so oblivious?* This realization did surprise me, but it didn't upset me; I just figured it might be time for me to take a different class since this one probably wasn't going to work out. The atmosphere, I had finally surmised, was thick with a seek-and-search for Mr. or Ms. right. I didn't want any part of that, but I did decide to stick around just a little longer. *Who knew? This would always make a great narrative in case I ever decided to write a book.*

I had two more months and many "social" adventures with that bunch before I decided to check back into Elmwood Playhouse. By that time, I needed a fix of reality, *or rehabilitation.* Either way, I knew that's exactly what the doctor would have ordered, and since I was not a big fan of psychiatrists, this was the preferred option. So, I walked right back into the next Monday night meeting of the Elmwood Players and it was just like old times. *I was home again.* As always, the minutes were read and discussed along with fundraising ideas, and there were a few follow-up questions. Eventually, the talk rolled back around to casting, and I sat up a little straighter to make sure my presence was noticed. The play *You Can't Take It with You* was to be performed at the next meeting, and they needed to cast for the lead role of Ed Carmichael.

You Can't Take It with You revolves around Ed Carmichael's life. He is a man with a printing press in his basement and a wife studying to become a dancer. There is plenty of chaos swirling around the Carmichael abode, including the threat of foreclosure of their very home itself! The play, a comedy of all things, had been a rollicking success on Broadway, and director Frank Capra brought the film version of the story to life in 1938. The movie won two Oscars for best picture and best director, and I was impressed by the accolades it had achieved.

Right after the meeting, one of the Elmwood members chatted with me and decided it would be a good idea to introduce me to the director. I was still only seventeen at this time, and I really was a little too young to play the part of a married man. But the director asked me a few questions about my availability and the rehearsal schedule. These posed no issues for me since rehearsals were all at night. *What better after school project could there be?* Despite my youth, and perhaps because she had faith in the power of theatrical makeup, the director gave me the starring role! *My first - I could not believe it and I was to the moon with joy!*

This time around, I knew enough to do my homework. It was, in fact, the only homework I didn't mind doing as it involved research in order to fully understand the character and what he was all about. Ed Carmichael was not a simple man, instead, he was quite a complex character. This, in turn, made my study trying to understand his motivations quite difficult but at the same time exciting. He is a husband to Essie, a son-in-law to Paul and Penny - a xylophone player, and he helps to distribute Essie's candies. As an amateur printer, he prints anything that sounds interesting to him, from dinner menus for his family to communist pamphlets that he places in the boxes of Essie's candy. Oh, and did I mention that he also likes to make masks?

I researched period clothing, and luckily, fashion trends in the mid 1970's were not that different from those of the 1930's. Ladies wore floral printed chiffon dresses and men sported pinstripe pants and shirts with rounded collars. Apparently, my clothes were quite fashionable for that time, and were very similar to what Ed himself would have worn, because the wardrobe director approved of a pair of my own pants and one of my own shirts.

Another coincidence which helped me get into Ed Carmichael's mindset was that I was studying graphic arts in school. My experience with a printing press allowed me to more easily relate to a man who would operate a printing press in his basement. These causal connections were further proof that I was in the right place at the right time. In fact, I began to feel like part of me was already Ed Carmichael, and this was great since I had not yet learned any methods of fully getting into character. *Knowing I was where I was meant to be* filled me with a natural high, so to speak. I felt I was going to deliver my best performance yet!

This time around, my parents and other family members would be coming to see me perform. I wanted to impress them with my skills as an actor, and more than that, I wanted them to see that this was truly my career calling. I didn't know what to expect as far as their reactions even if I should deliver a stellar performance. Having done my homework, giving it my all during the rehearsals, and learning by watching and listening to the other experienced actors, who guided me every step of the way, I thought I was about as ready as I could be.

You Can't Take It with You was my first ever evening-length play. I checked to see that my family had good seats and had actually shown up, and I felt confident and focused the night the production opened. I had learned to put my focus on my character, and once there, to never look back. Happy to say that I delivered a strong performance. My own sense of self-confidence soared, and the support I felt from the cast and director were powerful enough to make me certain that I would act again. Somehow, despite my anxiety beforehand, everything came together to make this production a successful one for me and for the Elmwood Playhouse.

"So, you're going to be an actor now?" Mom said after the show. We had gone to a nearby diner for coffee - most of my family and some of the cast and crew.

"What do you think?" I asked my mom and my dad.

"You did great! I couldn't believe that was you up there!" Mom said, not directly answering my question, but also not denying my acting potential.

My dad nodded in concurrence, and I felt elated to be getting such positive feedback from my parents.

It was sad when this particular performance ended, but I was always looking ahead, knowing that there would be other opportunities coming my way. For now, though, acting was put on the back burner while I became wrapped up in the traditions and hoopla surrounding high school graduation. First there was a rehearsal for commencement and then the excitement of the actual day of graduation. I had been looking forward to this occasion for quite some time, because, to me, it signified that I finally had the freedom and opportunity to chase my dreams. I sat in my chair on the football field dressed in the traditional cap and gown and waited for my name to be called. With over 400 graduates, there was a lot of waiting time. With a steady stride, I embarked across the recently posited temporary stage. I shook hands with the dignitaries, eagerly accepted my diploma, and made sure to turn and beam out into the audience. Though I wasn't playing a role that afternoon, walking across that stage felt comfortably familiar and it reminded me of where I wanted to go and what I intended to do with my life.

Before planning my next steps in my chosen career, I had prom to look forward to. I bought my first car, a blue 1966 Dodge Coronet, right before graduation, and I was proud to be driving it to the prom. My date was my good friend Liz, who had been my best pal throughout high school. By the way, she was, *and still is,* a beauty. My best friend Tony, and his date Debbie, would be going with us for the night's festivities. Tony had been my best friend since early childhood, and we were inseparable, more like brothers than best friends. We always had a good time when we were together, because he and I had a knack for creating good times out of nothing. I knew this night would be no different.

I felt a little stiff and uncomfortable in my brown tux when I first got dressed but being out with my best friends had relaxed me in no time. The prom was held at the Tappan Zee Inn, an upscale venue for a high school prom. We strolled through the sliding glass doors at the entrance and were amazed by the glamorous surroundings. Our dates' heels clicked across the gleaming marble floor as we made our way to the ballroom. The dance floor was bathed in swirling lights, there were stunning red and white floral arrangements on the buffet tables to reflect our school colors, and the sides of the room were draped in luxurious dupioni silk. I stood a little taller in my tux, trying to feel worthy of being a participant in an event within this stylish room.

We circulated around the room, enjoying the *mock*tail hour for a while, high-fiving and hugging our friends along the way. Then Tony gave me his mischievous nod, and the four of us headed back to the car to retrieve our prized bottle of rum. Since Tony had been responsible for scoring the booze, he had the honor of sneaking it back into the prom. He tucked the flat bottle into the waistband of his light blue tux for safekeeping. Unfortunately, though, his slight frame gave the bottle nothing to rest upon, and the bottle slid unceremoniously down his left pants leg before hitting the ground. All four of us let out a startled, "Ahh!" and then held our breath.

We just knew that the bottle had cracked, and its golden contents had wastefully spilled onto the asphalt of the parking lot. However, when Tony reached down to get it, somehow the bottle had survived the fall, and we let out a hoop and a holler when we realized that, almost miraculously, the bottle remained in one piece! We then decided not to risk another episode and so I stuffed it into my pants pocket, and we headed back inside. Thankfully, in those days in our small community, no guards were present to frisk us, scan us, or to pat us down in any way. *These were still the innocent times, ones that we will probably never see again, unfortunately.*

Well, I don't mind reporting that we enjoyed the best rum and cokes we had ever tasted! Prom was fun, but the best was yet to come at the after parties. First, we gathered at a local upscale restaurant where we indulged in even more food before moving on to the house of one of our friend's. The party there was an all-nighter and I had never had such a blast before then, never have since, and probably will never have as much fun again at any time going forward! It was such a blast getting all decked out and being surrounded by good friends, and don't think it never crossed my mind on more than one occasion that evening, that having such a great time might be what life would feel like in Hollywood.

And it just never stopped! The following day, the four of us headed to Seaside Heights, New Jersey, a beach destination about two hours from our home. We would be creating good times and memories of our own making at the Jersey Shore. Seaside has an amazing boardwalk crammed-full of arcades, carnival-like games of chance and skill, the most amazing rides, and of course, food of every description. We were young, free of life's trappings for the moment, and the world was our oyster, so to speak. We let ourselves soak in all the wondrous glories which life could offer. It seemed the sky was the limit with what we could achieve!

It wasn't until our excursion ended and I had had time to let my thoughts settle down from all of the excitement, that I began to focus once again on my chosen career. Even though I had been distracted by the chaos and joy of graduation, in the back of my mind, visions of Hollywood were never too far away. My dreams were like a constant temptation, occupying and flirting around inside my head. My goal was to become a popular actor with successful performances in tv, film, and on stage. I was sure that most people would think I was after the stardom, but truthfully, that wasn't what motivated me. Sure, Travolta had achieved both fame and a successful career, but I would be very satisfied with just a successful career. Stardom evokes the feeling of being loved by a large audience, but I wasn't after that and didn't need that kind of gratification. I only wanted to know that I had performed well.

Once my schedule resumed its normal routine, the next ritual of a young man's life took precedence. I had graduated high school, and it was now time for me to work on a full-time basis - financial obligations soon took hold since I did not want to be known as a freeloader.

Since the age of sixteen, I had worked as a busboy and waiter at the Rockland Country Club. The past two summers while I had still been in high school found me practicing my manners while waiting on paying customers. This was tough work no matter what they tell you. You have to be fast and efficient; but more important than that, you have to make sure to keep up with the boss's expectations. I would wind up working there for five years until that job ended abruptly. The truth is, I was fired for no good reason. That was fine with me, because I had learned that what happens at the country club *doesn't necessarily stay at the country club*, and that, let's just say… *is a story for a different kind of book.*

And so, I took a job at the shipping department at Becton Dickinson Diagnostics in 1982. The good thing about that job was that it kept my nights and weekends free. Three years had quickly passed, and at the age of twenty-one, I finally felt secure, and the idea of stability was not such a bad thing. I was happy that my new job was reliable, but the pay wasn't that great. More than any of those things; however, was the strong desire to return to the theater coming back to wallop me over the head big-time.

I woke up one morning and realized that now was the time for me to make a career out of acting. I had little to lose, and I had known deep down that I could never turn away for good from this calling. So, I knew there was only one thing for me to do ... *the following week, I returned home to the Elmwood Playhouse's Monday night meetings.*

***

Chapter Three

Angela

***

When the next Monday night rolled around, I was once again in my familiar theater seat, looking up at Walter on the Elmwood Playhouse stage. He was busy scrutinizing the paper which outlined the night's schedule. As I sat there just enjoying the atmosphere of the old theater - the cushioned seats of the auditorium, the overhead lights in the catwalk above the stage, the wooden floor of the stage itself, with the backdrop of a painted garden replete with a gazebo and a footbridge over a small pond - I realized that I somehow felt completely at home inside this playhouse in a way that was both comforting and exciting. The Elmwood stage did not have curtains and so the set design for the upcoming production was always the backdrop for the meetings. The aforementioned painted garden was the set design for the upcoming production of *The Boy Friend.*

My experiences at Elmwood had thus far served me well and as I reminisced about my first few experiences here, I knew they had helped me focus, *and sometimes refocus*, on my goal of becoming a gifted and able actor. I had lost time these past five years in frivolous endeavors which had taken me away from my dreams. Now, I wanted acting to be my career and not just a hobby, and I knew I needed to keep taking steps forward in order to make that happen - *even if they were baby steps and even if they only came few and far*

60

between. The Elmwood group had the unique ability to both ground me and push me out of my comfort zone. It was a safe place to try my hand at new skills, and though I didn't know it as I sat in my familiar seat at the start of this evening's meeting, what I was about to experience in my near future would certainly stretch my abilities.

I surveyed the room and saw quite a few familiar faces, along with some new ones. Sitting right next to me that night was a woman who resembled Angela Lansbury: her short graying hair and round face were complimented by large brown eyes which twinkled with a motherly effervescence. She was overdressed in a light green blouse, gray slacks, and expensive red walking shoes, and I wondered if she had dressed for a certain part in this evening's brief theatrical scene. Anyway, she was a new face to me, and so I introduced myself.

"Hello, I'm Tom Stratford. I did some work in the theater about five years ago."

She scrutinized me up and down and otherwise just gazed into my eyes with a certain, familiar kind of reverie. When she did not introduce herself, I stretched out my arm to shake hands and, probably because I was a bit nervous, I continued telling her my life story. "Even though it's been a while, honestly, I am very motivated. Although I have just a little experience, I'm hoping to get some more training here."

She never introduced herself by name, but she shook my hand and gave me a warm and gentle smile. I will call her *Angela*. "Believe me, we are all actors in training," Angela said to me, allowing her hand to linger a bit longer in mine. "Continuing to hone our craft is something all good actors do; you don't need to feel alone in that regard." Her words made sense to me, and once again confirmed the fact that I had made a good decision in returning to the Elmwood Playhouse. Turning her attention back to the stage, she whispered, "Looks like we will be starting the meeting soon."

Following Walter's reading of last week's minutes, he introduced himself to those in the audience in order to welcome the new faces. Next, came information about a rise in ticket prices, needed construction on the roof, and a plea for everyone to update their contact information. Soon, Walter finished sharing the business details for the night and finally came to the one thing I had been waiting for, information about their upcoming production.

The Boy Friend, as it turned out, was a full-length, period musical written in 1954. A parody of popular 1920's romantic comedies, the musical takes place in France and follows the dream of a young heiress searching for a boyfriend. Paramount to the musical, was, of course, plenty of singing and dancing numbers; neither skill being one which I had currently possessed. And so, when Walter announced that one of three *chorus boys* had suddenly dropped out of rehearsals and they were in need of an immediate replacement, I did not raise my hand to volunteer. As much as I wanted to get back on stage, I felt like not having any experience with dancing or singing would be a definite deal-breaker; *I knew my limitations.*

So, I decided that it would be best if I waited a short time until the next project was announced before getting involved with a production again. I did feel a little disappointed, but I knew I had no business pretending to be ready for a musical. *However, Angela felt differently.* She nudged my forearm with her bony elbow, "Go on," she encouraged, "you can do it." She looked at me with a mischievous smile and then nodded her head in the direction of the stage. I grabbed my forearm protectively and answered, "Thanks for the vote of confidence, but I don't have much experience with dancing and singing. I think I am going to have to sit this one out. I'll get involved in the next one."

Obviously, she had no reservations about me taking the part of the chorus boy at all! Her elbow nudged me again, this time with a rather forceful nudge into my ribcage. "Oh, don't be so silly," she said. "We need somebody and that's all there is to it. You have the looks and the charm, and so you're our likely candidate. You're an actor, just the right age, *and you can become anyone you need to be.*"

I glanced at Walter, who was still waiting for someone from the audience to respond. Turning, I did not see any likely candidates. Angela took this as a sign that she was winning her argument with me. I didn't even have the time to realize I was in an argument before she harped on the opportunity. "*See?* Look around, you don't see anyone else volunteering, do you? " When I did not respond, and judging by the concerned look on my face, she knew she had won. With that, she grabbed my arm and hoisted me out of my seat, dragging me along with her up to the stage, making a beeline for the director, who was seated adjacent to Walter's chair. "Let's get this taken care of right away," she crooned. I felt like a schoolboy being chastised by a gym teacher for not having completed the rope climb. However, I reluctantly trudged behind her, and the next thing I knew, I was face-to-face with the director.

I protested against the very idea of considering me for the role by highlighting my lack of experience singing and dancing, but this did not seem to matter to

Kate Levin Farren, the director. In fact, she didn't ask any questions at all about my previous experience. She simply took one look at me and then thanked Angela effusively for having introduced us. "Looks like we have our new chorus boy," she exclaimed to no one in particular, but everyone heard her just the same. I believe I blushed a bit in response, and to me, she merely said, "Thanks for volunteering. We have no time to waste, *so your rehearsals will start tomorrow night.*"

What? Had I heard her correctly? Seeing her bright blue eyes staring at me, I realized she was waiting for some kind of a euphoric reaction from me. I managed to say, "Sure," and then I shook her hand. "Happy to help," I stated, trying to sound confident and routine, but I am almost positive that my voice reflected the shock and uncertainty I was feeling.

The reality was that in no time at all, I had become the newest member of the cast of *The Boy Friend*, this time a chorus boy named Marcel. I knew I was underqualified, and I had lots of doubts about how I was going to pull this off, but what choice did I have? *Hey - Travolta had expanded his repertoire of skills going from Vinnie Barbarino to Danny Zuko in Grease, hadn't he?* They needed me and I needed to be on stage - that was the bottom line. If Travolta had done it, I would do it! After mingling and meeting a few other cast members of *The Boy Friend*, I eagerly made my way back up the carpeted aisle toward the exit.

I walked out of the Elmwood Playhouse doors that night floating on air, and nothing else, except perhaps the tiny bit of nervousness accompanying my burgeoning doubts. *What had I done? I'm gonna fall flat up there on stage, I'm gonna make a fool of myself!* As I got in my car, wouldn't you know it - the song playing on my favorite radio station was *"You're the One That I Want,"* from *Grease.* Travolta and Olivia Newton-John at their finest! The more I thought about it, I started to calm down. I put the car in gear and began tapping my fingers on the steering wheel to the beat of the duet's crooning. *How difficult can the singing and acting be if they were so eager to overlook my inexperience?* I began singing along to Travolta's part, and hell, then Olivia's part, as well. *Not bad! I can do this.* By the time I got home, I was crooning out each of the tunes coming from my car's radio. I had convinced myself I would be the next greatest *chorus boy* the stage had ever seen! *To my heart, I must be true ....*

But first, I knew I had to take the correct next steps forward. In the coming days, I woke up each morning thinking not about my workday, but about the evening ahead. My job at the diagnostic company was a traditional nine-to-five, which worked well for me because it meant I had my evenings free to rehearse. Before I even attended my first rehearsal, I knew that I would have some catching up to do, but I didn't realize exactly how far behind I would be and how much help I would need.

It only took that first rehearsal to make it very clear that I needed to get some quick vocal and dance training. During the chorus numbers, I did my best to sing along; however, my voice sounded way off key, even to myself. I struggled to find the right tone and to follow the tune, but my voice seemed tight and constricted when it was supposed to bend and flow. One of my ideas was to hide just how bad I was singing by barely letting any sound at all flow from my mouth. *I mouthed the words silently.* Sometimes, I even covered my mouth with the song sheet I had to hold while learning the music. Luckily, no one seemed to notice, and no one called me out, even the director Kate. *Was she just being nice for now?* My insecurity with my role in singing made my nerves go haywire, *and then we started the dance numbers.*

Well ... when I compared my dancing to my singing skills, *my dance skills were even worse, if you can imagine that.* Everyone else had most of the movements down, and their routines seemed effortless and focused. I noticed all of their smooth transitions within the various parts to each of the numbers. *My focus was my feet.* Every step I took, my feet felt like heavy sandbags. No matter how hard I tried to move them quickly, *they failed me.* I must have tripped over myself a hundred times, and even though all I needed to do was to follow the lead of the chorus boy in front of me, I could not move in the proper direction to save my life. If I anticipated we would move to the right, he'd go left, and when I thought we should bow into a slow spin, suddenly he was hopping up and down across the stage. When the choreographer ended rehearsals that night, I was grateful to make a quick getaway.

Mastering the skills I would need to perform this role with justice was not going to come easily. That night, I looked in the classified section of the newspaper for someone offering singing lessons, thinking I would tackle one skill at a time and singing was less intimidating to me. Sure enough, there were two ads: one for a male about my age and the other for a female who was a good bit older. Since I needed to gain some confidence and I needed to do it in a hurry, I chose the female, believing that she would have amassed enough experience to be an effective vocal coach for someone at my beginner's level.

I met with my vocal coach, Jayme Smalley, the following afternoon, squeezing in a lesson between my day job and rehearsal at the Playhouse. She asked me to sing one of the pieces from *The Boy Friend*. Reluctantly, I began, but she cut me off after just a few notes. "Well," she said, looking at me with a pleasant but somewhat condescending smile. "We've got some work to do, but I think I can get you where you need to be. We'll have no time to waste, though." Her confidence gave me confidence. For the next hour, I practiced singing notes that mirrored the ones she sang, I learned to sing from the depths of my diaphragm, and by the end of the lesson, I surprised myself with an increased ability to stay in tune. Before leaving that first lesson, I made plans with Jayme to meet again for the next several days in a row.

After a little more of this vocal work, I was beginning to hold my own during our rehearsals with my fledgling singing abilities, but the dancing was another story altogether. The choreographer for the production was a former schoolmate and friend of mine named Peter and let me tell you - *Peter loved his work.* Like Busby Berkeley, the famous American director and choreographer, Peter enjoyed crafting intricate dance numbers with oversized props and large casts. From his perch high on top of a ladder, Peter would look down at the dancers and vigorously wave his yardstick around, directing dancers this way and that. He was like the queen bee, or mother hen, and he shouted corrections with a voice that could be heard above the roar of the music, always demanding faster footwork and smoother transitions.

There were two big dance numbers for *The Boy Friend* which required my involvement. One of them included dancing the tango at a costume party. To add insult to injury, it wasn't just my feet that were a problem. My costume for the dance numbers was similar to that of an Aladdin character, and on my head, I had to balance a giant yellow headdress/mask. It was a bizarre-looking joker face straight out of something you would see on Bourbon Street during Mardi Gras. The face had a wide and devilish, red-mouthed grin, the nose was long and sinewy, and the entire thing was covered in fake jewels. The first time I leaned over and picked it up, I was shocked by how heavy it was; its features stretched out to cover an area that was three of my own-sized heads. When I put it on, I immediately realized that such a weighted headdress made my neck feel more like spaghetti noodles than muscle.

Not only did I have my headpiece to get used to, but the dance steps themselves continued to be a clear and present challenge. This was the tango, and the footwork was fast and intricate, combining three altogether different motions within one move. When I was supposed to be moving in a circular direction, I could only manage linear movement. When I was supposed to be sashaying to the left, I could only march stiffly. Although I felt embarrassed by my lack of skill, I was quite surprised by how little my dance mates complained. Once in a while, I would strain my neck upward to see Queen Peter on top of his ladder waving that infamous yardstick faster and faster. "Get lower!" he yelled. *"Lower!"* His eyes were trained on me.

And so, I bent my knees and tried my best to get lower, but every movement made my headdress shift precariously. I felt like I would soon fall head-first into the stage. Sensing Peter's eyes drilling holes into my brain right through the headdress, I hunched my shoulders, hoping that would give the impression that I was going lower. *Nope!* "Get lower still," he cried, "Or I am coming down off of this ladder *(i.e, his perch or throne!)* and I will crack some kneecaps!" To make his point, he slammed his yardstick into the palm of his free hand. *Smack!*

Peter's criticisms were directed mainly at me, and really, I couldn't blame him. I just could not get my footwork right nor master the elaborate patterns of movement which were necessary. Soon, his assistant pulled me out of the formation and dragged me off to a private area while the rest of the cast continued onto the next number. Minute after minute, the assistant counted out the dance steps for me and had me continuously repeating the patterns. My feet had no trouble getting tangled up in one another, and my frustration was peaking. *I had told them I wasn't a dancer, and even now they weren't throwing me off the show. I guess they really were desperate for fresh talent like me. Could it have been that cool Travolta-like charm I exuded?*

Well, minutes soon turned into hours, and finally, I began to make progress. As I learned the routine, my steps grew more fluid, and I was able to pick up the pace. The sandbags at the bottom of my legs started feeling quite a bit lighter, but in the meantime, the headdress was still like a luxury-liner anchor covering my head. As a safety measure, I began using my arms to balance my headpiece every time the assistant looked in the other direction. I was determined to learn what was necessary, if only because I was interested in seeing Peter attempt to come down off his shaky wooden pedestal and then crack *anything* with his yardstick. That would be a sight I would not have wanted to miss for the world!

Eventually, the assistant stopped having to count out each beat, and he began to back away from me, watching me from across the room rather than sticking close to my side. My feet ached and sweat poured down my face, but even as tired as I was, I was beginning to feel a little pride in my work. At the end of that night's rehearsal, the assistant declared that I could rejoin the cast at our next rehearsal. *I had done it.* Maybe I would never be anything more than an adequate dancer, but it seemed that I could do enough to get by, and at this point, *that was all that mattered to me.*

The following week was opening night. I felt that unbelievable excitement which all actors get when they are moments away from a performance. As I stood in the wings, the musical unfolded before my very own eyes. Several actors faltered a bit here and there: there were some forgotten lines and missed cues, but I doubted that the audience had noticed any of those things. As it got close to my time on stage, my heartbeat sped up, and I could feel my knees getting a little shaky. There was already sweat beading on my forehead, and I hadn't even put on the headdress! Knowing that I was the least experienced singer and dancer of the entire cast, I was hoping that my work, and all that extra training, would serve me well enough once I took the stage. I dressed in my costume, donned the headdress, and soon enough, I heard the music that signaled my entrance.

Without thinking twice about it, I danced out onto the stage, headdress and all.

It wasn't a perfect performance. My nerves had caused me to miss a step or two but my feet had somehow managed to follow the assigned dance steps with only a few mistakes. But my greatest surprise was that the gleaming yellow headdress had somehow managed to stay balanced on my head. Overall, I finished my part feeling satisfied enough and surprised that I could move rather well on stage. *Hey - I could even carry a tune!* There had been plenty of laughter and applause from the audience which, to me, meant there were indications that as shaky as opening night might have been, it had been a success in the eyes of those watching. Sure enough, the reviews which followed were positive, and every single future performance ended up selling out.

I felt gratified and very relieved that I was able to pull off working in a musical, and as our performances continued, I knew I was getting better with each performance, *one step* at a time. As my two new skills improved, I was able to relax a bit more and enjoy the experience as we went along. This was wonderful and boosted my confidence, especially considering that the overall experience of singing and dancing had felt so foreign at the start. Then something happened during our run of *The Boy Friend* which made the show even more of a success for me, personally, and that was when a director who had also seen my performance in *You Can't Take It with You* approached me and asked me to audition *for the next* Elmwood production. *Wow! Talk about an ego booster!* Being sought out to act reinforced for me the idea that I was back on track to being a successful actor. It was a groundbreaking experience for me to have been chosen for a role based upon a past performance, *and I was ecstatic.*

Elmwood's next production would be

Philadelphia Here I Come, a dramatic play about the

character Garth, a young man who was planning to leave

his hometown in Ireland and move to Philadelphia to

start a new life in America. As it turned out, I was

offered the part of one of Garth's friends, but instead, I

wanted the part of Joe, the youngest of Garth's friends,

because it was a smaller role. I had made this decision

because I was still working full-time and I was still

focused on continuing to dance the tango with that

ridiculously heavy headdress in *The Boy Friend,* which

would be continuing at the same time rehearsals for

Philadelphia would begin. I auditioned for the part of

Joe, the friend who was most torn by Garth's moving to

America, and who could not understand why Garth was

leaving his friends and family behind. *I got the role of*

Joe! Taking the smaller role was the smart move for me

at the time, after all, the last thing I needed was another big challenge to distract me from singing in tune and hitting my dance steps adequately!

Getting cast in *Philadelphia* quickly became an amazing opportunity for me due to the fact that I was able to learn from an incredible director, Denise Beckerle. She was truly a Godsend. For the first time, I actually felt like I was being taught to act. Denise was easy to get along with but also serious about her directing. Almost every day, she pointed out subtle, but significant, changes that I could make to improve my timing and delivery. I learned how pauses could be used as effective tools, and how important the pacing and tone of my words can be. She taught me where to focus my eyes and how to move my body according to the context. A shrug of my shoulder or nod of my chin became gestures for expression that went beyond my words and voice. She also emphasized how important it was to connect with my character; since I understood what she was trying to achieve, I was entirely motivated to listen to her direction, learn from it, and then follow through.

Once *The Boy Friend* closed after its successful run, I was happy to be able to devote my full attention to *Philadelphia* and my character Joe. We only had two weeks before our newest production would begin, and I tried taking advantage of those last rehearsals to the fullest of my ability. On opening night, I was eager to put all that I had learned into practice. I knew that I had grown as an actor under Denise's tutelage, and I could not wait to try out all of my newest techniques and skills - I wanted to make myself proud and this entire performance a rollicking success.

In one particular scene, my character was the last of Garth's friends to tell him goodbye before he left for

America. From studying my character, I understood that as Joe, I had conflicting emotions: I was losing a great friend, but I understood why he needed to go. I saw their relationship as complex and playing out through a multitude of levels. During this scene, I thought about having to say goodbye to one of my own friends in order to tap into a similar painful experience of loss. *But maybe I was saying goodbye to someone who meant more to me than only just a friend.*

I saw Garth standing there before me. My shoulders slumped sadly, and my voice quivered with emotion as I reached out to give him a heartfelt goodbye handshake, and the tears in my eyes that opening night were real. It was like all of the pent-up feelings I had conjured during our rehearsals for this scene had finally been let loose. Suddenly, I felt the quiet hush of the audience, and I knew I had captured a poignant moment.

I could not stop myself - I reacted to the energy coming my way from them. The handshake spontaneously turned into an emotional embrace and Garth wrapped me in his arms. We both knew that the audience was completely hooked, overtaken with the moment. Each of them in their own way could relate to the feelings of losing someone they loved, *and now they were doing so through the eyes of a character I had brought to life.*

The show received outstanding reviews and was a great success. We were all so happy and glad for the hard work which we had put in under Denise's direction. Now, I look back on that time as one of my all-time favorite experiences. Not only had I learned so much about timing, character study, and stage presence, but I realized it was Denise's direction itself which had been critical in making my performance as good as it had become. This was, arguably, the most important realization of my entire acting career up until that time. *It would soon lead me to one of my most cherished mentors.*

Once I understood the power of learning from another whose skills were fine-honed through a lifetime of bettering their craft, it seemed that life itself began contributing to my calling as an actor by showing me the way. One night backstage before another performance of *Philadelphia*, I overheard the lead actor talking to Denise about his acting coach and his membership in AFTRA, a television union for actors. *Wait. This guy, an established actor already, has an acting coach? Why didn't I think about that?* I had a million questions for him, for instance, *can I get into this union?*

I waited until he was through talking with Denise, and then I approached him. "So, Jim," I said. "Did I hear correctly that you have an acting coach? I think that I could use one myself."

"Of course, I do," Jim responded, as if my question itself was silly. "Whoever wants to take acting seriously should have a good coach."

I nodded eagerly. *"Who do you use?"*

He smiled and shook his head. "Uh-uh, I don't share that information with anyone. If I told you, I would have to kill you."

Just like an actor to state something so dramatically! I stood there uncertain what to say next.

But being a good sport, Jim bailed me out. "You need to do some research and find somebody you are comfortable to work with, especially if you plan on making a career out of this."

I nodded enthusiastically. "Of course! I'll do that," I said, not knowing exactly how or where I'd find someone, but then again, *I reaffirmed for myself that not knowing something had never stopped me before.*

"Thanks for the tip."

He began walking away and I felt an urgency, not wanting to wait for the answer to my other question. "Oh, and Jim?" He stopped and turned back to face me somewhat impatiently. "What is this AFTRA and would I be able to join?"

"Sure," he answered. "It's the best television union for actors. *You have to join* if you're serious about acting as a career. Come see me after the show and I'll give you the number to call."

I called AFTRA the following day and scheduled a time to drive into New York City to fill out the application right in their offices. Then, I began my search for an appropriate acting coach. I asked other actors and Denise, I looked at flyers and business cards tacked to cork boards, I scoured local newspapers and bulletins. Nothing stood out or called to me at first. I also made another decision I believed was necessary if I was serious about making acting my career.

It seemed like common sense, and everyone knew that actors must endure lengthy periods of low income if they are to finally get their break; it's customary. I would have to literally starve if I wanted this bad enough, to show that no matter what else, I was working hard doing bit parts but holding out for that big break. If I wanted to commit myself fully to becoming successful, I could do no less. So, after three years of working at Becton Dickinson Diagnostics, I quit my job and took a less demanding and less time-consuming job at the nearby, popular Italian restaurant *Villa Venice*. I knew that I would be making significantly less money, but that I would have more time to devote to my profession. This was the path I believed most serious actors took, and at this time in my life, I was much more focused on achieving my dream than I was concerned about achieving financial stability.

By now, it was 1985, and I had officially become a member of AFTRA, but so far, I had little success finding anyone I considered to be a good match to fulfill the role as my acting coach. I remained determined nonetheless, and one day, it occurred to me that I had found a great vocal coach through the county newspaper, and so I decided to go back and scour the classified ads in that rag once again. I had looked here before but there was only one person listed at the time and the face in his photo seemed too young for me to take him seriously.

It was a Monday afternoon, and I was in Nyack. I bought the paper from the local newsstand and then went to sit and have a cup of coffee at my favorite coffee shop, where I would occasionally splurge with one of their homemade hot buns. I opened the paper and turned immediately to the classifieds. A new ad caught my eye at once - she was from West Nyack (the small city adjoining Nyack only miles away) and had experience in Hollywood. The bottom line of the ad stated: *"Acting coach. For all ages. For information call Elmwood 8 1611."* She was offering herself as an acting coach and the ad referred to an article about her in *The Hollywood Reporter,* a magazine all about Hollywood and its stars.

Finishing my coffee, I ran across the street and down Broadway Avenue to the Nyack Library, knowing they carried this magazine. Sure enough, they had this issue available. I sat at one of the tables and flipped through the pages until I saw a photo of a beautiful and elegant young actress from the thirties. Something about the sparkle in her eyes showed great wisdom. The article talked about her acting career, went on to list all of her roles, and it discussed her popularity at great lengths. It said she was now retired from acting, was living in West Nyack, NY, and had become a teacher of the acting craft. I looked at her photo once again and something about her drew me in and made me feel like we were long lost relatives.

Her name was Zita Johann, and I could not wait to get home and give her a call. *Zita Johann seemed to be just what I was looking for ....*

***

Chapter Four

Elmwood 8

***

My instincts told me that finding Zita Johann, *a well-known actress who lived in the area and was now coaching other aspiring actors,* seemed to me to be more than just coincidental. Perhaps due to my overriding sense of confidence that I was meant to be an actor, I truly believed I was now on the right track to finding the success I sought, and I had no doubt that reaching out to her would be the right move. *This is going to take my talent to the next level.* From my research about her thus far, I knew that she had an impressive career, and I was excited about the possibility of working with someone so accomplished. So, without hesitation, I held the newspaper ad in my hand and dialed her number. I thought it interesting that dialing the number starting with *Elmwood 8* would lead me to Zita. Elmwood 8 was *EL8,* or the 358 prefix for the Nyack area.

"Hello," Zita's warm voice sang out through the telephone line.

"Ms. Johann," I replied, "my name is Tom Stratford, and I am calling in reference to your ad about coaching actors. I was hoping that you are accepting new students at this time."

"Wonderful," she replied. Her voice was friendly and firm. "You have called at a good time, because I do have room for one more student. But Tom," she cautioned, " I never take on a student without meeting him or her in person."

I was a little concerned by her request, *what would this initial interview be all about?* I quickly recovered. "That's not a problem at all," I responded. "I would be happy to meet with you at your convenience."

"I hope you understand," she continued. "I take my work seriously, and I think it is important that the match between teacher and student is a good one. Meeting first allows me to learn about you and your goals so that we can make sure we are a good fit for one another."

"Of course," I answered. I liked her direct approach, and I appreciated the fact that she seemed serious about forming an appropriate mentorship. Well, *I was serious about upping my game, too!* As I thought more about it, I realized this would protect both of us, since I would be getting to know her a little bit, as well; and of course, I did not want to risk wasting my time or my money on someone who could not help me.

"Another thing, Tom," she mentioned, less formally. "As it turns out, I am appearing on *The Joe Franklin Show* tonight to talk about a book I have just finished writing. Why don't you tune in? It might give you some good insight about me before we meet."

I was immediately excited by the prospect of actually seeing her in action as a movie star. *"I'll certainly do that,"* I responded. With that, we agreed to meet at her house and set the date for the following day. I carefully wrote down the directions to her home address as she spoke them to me and they seemed clear enough. I hung up the phone *(think old school here: no tap of a red button to end the call, but an actual telephone attached by a cord to its base which one needed to place back in its cradle to end the call!).*

Filled with great expectations and hopeful anticipation for the next step forward in my acting career, I took a deep breath and smiled to myself. Zita Johann seemed to me like just the kind of coach/instructor/mentor I needed - genuine but no nonsense, professional and with scruples. *I couldn't wait to see her on TV that night and then meet her in person the following day!*

Early that evening, I stood at the kitchen sink helping my mom with the dinner dishes. She washed them and I used the cotton dishcloth to dry our dishes. My mind had not strayed far from my conversation with Zita, and I was eager to share my excitement. I dried the last dinner plate and put it into the cupboard before sitting back down at the kitchen table, where dessert was waiting. My mom is a great baker, and in fact, that is a skill I am happy to say I inherited from her. On this particular night, she had made a chocolate cake and its glossy, deep-brown, frosting beckoned me. Ending our already robust meal with a delicious slice of her rich and delicious cake, together with a hot cup of freshly brewed coffee, was just about as enticing to me at that moment as the news I was about to share.

It was just the two of us in the kitchen at the moment. The others had taken a break to stretch their legs, use the bathroom, catch the news, and so on. "So, Mom," I said, " I have some news to share. I am going to work with an acting coach."

She lifted her eyes towards me, which had been focused prior to that on slicing the cake in perfect sections. "Well, that seems like a logical step. But how are you going to find one?"

I broke out into a confident smile as she handed

me a piece of cake, "I already have! Her name is Zita

Johann. Do you recognize that name?" I raised my fork

and dug into a little bit of heaven.

"Oh, have you? No - I can't say that I do. Tell me

about her. How did you find her?" Her voice resonated

with a keen interest in my news, laced with just a pinch

of precaution.

I pulled out Zita's ad from my pocket and handed

it to her. "She was in, like, seven movies in the 1930's,

including the original *The Mummy* with Boris Karloff -

she was his love interest, *remember that one?* She was

also in Edward G. Robinson's *Tiger Shark.*" Mom did

not respond and so I just continued. "I'm so lucky! She

lives in West Nyack, so this will be really convenient. I

read a big article about her in *The Hollywood Reporter* at

the library, and she had an amazing career. I've already

spoken with her on the phone and she sounds fantastic - we've agreed to meet. *Anyway, I think I can learn a lot from her."*

"Okay, Tommy. If that's what you think you should do." Mom smiled at me, which I took as affirmation that I was onto something with this new plan of action.

"Oh! *I almost forgot!* She just finished writing a book and is going to be on *The Joe Franklin Show* tonight. Why don't you watch it with me?" *The Joe Franklin Show* was a very popular syndicated show out of New York City at the time. Joe Franklin himself was known as one of the best and most entertaining talk show hosts and his show aired on New York's local WOR-TV. He would interview the most popular figures of both the past and present, and his show ran for many years.

"Okay, *let's see what you're getting into,*" Mom said.

I eagerly gobbled up the remaining bit of my cake, washed it down with her splendid coffee, then helped my mom put away the last of our dishes, and we headed to the living room. I turned the knob on the television just in time to catch Joe Franklin introducing Zita. He was a stout and robust man heading into his later years, balding just a bit on the top, but was full of zest and charm. "Well, now, I am pleased to bring out my next guest. She has earned many stage and film credits and has just recently written a book. Please, help me welcome actress Zita Johann."

I took the recliner while mom sat on the couch and we watched with great interest. As the studio audience applauded, a vibrant woman dressed stylishly in a dark green skirt with a matching jacket sashayed onto the studio stage with a confident smile lighting her face. Her appearance was reminiscent of the 1960's but it worked for her. She made immediate eye contact with the camera, inviting the audience into her world, and then she shook hands with Joe, a large black purse dangling from the crook of her arm. I thought it odd that she carried her purse on stage and I knew there must be a story to that, but for now, I could only imagine what it would be. Though almost eighty years old, she still had a commanding presence, with porcelain skin, dazzling brown eyes, and a neatly coiffed hairstyle which framed her face.

With a flourish, she waved her arm toward the audience and gave a slight bow in appreciation for their welcoming applause. At once, I was harkened back to the dramatic gestures performed by many of the famous actors who had become stars during the golden age of

Hollywood. *There was just something about their presence, how they commanded an audience and the stage....*

Joe Franklin motioned for Zita to have a seat, and she perched daintily on the edge of the upholstered chair, leaning slightly toward the host. She crossed one foot over the other and tilted her head to the side. "Zita, I have been looking forward to this interview for weeks now. I am so glad you have finally joined us!"

"Yes, well, Joe - you see, the timing is right at this point."

He nodded and otherwise seemed uncertain about how to respond for just a slight moment.

She was ready, though, and continued after just a perfect beat. *"At my age, Joe, it's all about the timing!"*

The audience erupted into laughter and Joe, himself relieved, found her response quite hysterical. The ice now broken, Joe went on to discuss her first film with Boris Karloff, *The Mummy.*

"He was a consummate professional." Zita said. "Never a wasted take - I would study his mannerisms and his focus. You see, you must be willing to learn from the best and to never challenge their wisdom."

"Yes, I would imagine that is great advice for all of us, in general, Zita!" Joe remarked.

I looked at my mom, who seemed to be engrossed in their conversation. *This was amazing!*

He followed up with questions about her acting career, praising her ability to capture characters in such detail and to take on roles in a way that sometimes surprised, yet delighted, directors and audiences alike. As the host peppered her with questions, Zita answered with a sweet voice that charmed the audience. Her face constantly registered a balance between wide-eyed innocence, laced with just the right amount of occasional thoughtfulness. *Sometimes she looked a bit uncertain, but I would not say she looked confused, but perhaps, she showed just a bit of hesitancy ....* The longer I watched, it became obvious to me that she was anything but confused. *She relished discussing her past once she had gotten over her initial concerns.*

Thinking about our brief phone conversation earlier along with the information I had gleaned from the article I had read, something told me that Zita was a strong-willed, confident woman who had various roles to play, each serving its own purpose.

Joe then asked Zita to describe her recent book, *After the End.* Although he was curious about her goal in writing the book, Zita discussed the setting of the story itself: an old hotel lounge, and the cast of characters - people trying to understand their situation and what got them there. There was something mystical and purposefully unclear in her description, as if she was saying, *you'll have to read it to know what it's all about, and why it was important for me to write it.*

He quickly moved on to finish with asking her what she thought about Hollywood itself. Zita discussed her time out on the West Coast in mostly unpleasant circumstances, and her preference for live theater over films as to why she had decided to devote herself to life in New York. And just like that, the seven-minute interview spot ended, and I watched Joe shake her hand and wish Zita continued success. She smiled and waved to me … *to the audience,* I mean, and with that, the show came to a close.

I was impressed with Zita. She was articulate, opinionated, and charming. It was clear to me that she had a lot to offer in terms of teaching an apprentice about what it takes to be a great actor, and I was excited to have the chance to work with her. Even my mom seemed impressed that I was going to rub elbows with someone so talented and famous. "Well, good luck," my mom said, smiling at me as she got up and made her way to the stairs, where she stopped and turned back for just an instant. "She seems nice enough, and I'm sure you will tell me all about her."

"Yes," I answered. "Can you believe I am actually going to be seeing her tomorrow? She seems incredibly talented. I'm very excited about meeting her."

"Sounds great, Tommy," Mom replied. "Oh, and close the windows before you come up. It looks like it might rain tonight."

I said, "Okay," as she headed upstairs.

My mom was never effusive with her praise or compliments, but I could tell that she was somewhat excited for me. *At least the doubts she had about my career choice in the beginning seem to have faded away.* As I reached to close a few windows, I could feel the spring chill in the night air. I turned off the lights and the TV, and the night instantly grew dark and still - the only sound I could hear was the occasional car passing by and my own heart beating strongly within my chest.

The next morning, as I headed out for my first meeting with Zita, I noticed that the spring rain from the night before had done its job. The green of the grass and trees was vibrant and deep, and the countryside teemed with fields of newborn life. Eighteen miles north of New York City was, at this time, still the country. Behind the wheel of my car, I noticed the beauty surrounding me and this seemed to reflect my own feelings of hope and promise. Zita's home was only three miles away from my parents' home, and I drove those miles with confidence. I was sure that today was going to be a milestone.

As I finished the short trek to Zita's house, though, there was only one problem. I could not find the driveway *or even see a house at all.* I had followed Zita's directions, which I had made certain to write precisely. She had said, "It is the last driveway on the right before the one-way tunnel." The tunnel that Zita had referred to lay below a train track which had not been traveled upon in many, many years. In fact, it was no longer an active part of the roadway and was now covered completely in clingy vines and green overgrowth. It would have been indistinguishable from a patch of woods, except for the exposed rocks forming a large U-shape above the old road.

Not just once or twice, but four times, I drove by the tunnel looking for an active roadway, path, or paved area while searching for Zita's driveway. *There was nothing in sight!* Finally, I decided to turn into the only driveway I could find, where I would take my chances, but almost immediately, I knew this wasn't right because it led to a modernly-styled home set in a wooded area. Zita's house, on the other hand, *or so she had told me,* was an old Revolutionary War house. And so there I was, running out of options and not knowing what else to do, rolling to a stop at the front of this driveway, staring at a beautiful, freshly built house and wondering *why had I even expected clear directions from a seventy-nine-year-old?*

Immediately, I saw an elderly woman's face staring at me from an open window to the side of the front door. *"Can I help you?"* she asked.

"I hope so," I replied. " I am hopelessly lost and looking for Zita Johann's place."

"Oh, yes, *Zita,*" she replied, and I was half-expecting her to burst out laughing - *another Hollywood wannabe calling on Zita to help them become the next biggest thing on two legs!* But the woman remained almost too kind and gentle, which worried me, as if she was trying to keep from giving away anything about what might lay ahead for me and Zita. "Her house is down the next driveway over." She pointed toward the woods and I finally saw a predominantly hidden structure deep within the trees and brush off the main road.

I pointed towards it. *"That one there?"* I was running late and I wanted to find Zita's, and I hoped that this would turn out to be her house. On the other hand, if it were to be Zita's house, an entirely new set of worries took hold over me: visions of *The Addams Family* home sifted through my memories.

Sure enough, the lady smiled softly and nodded. *"Yes, that's the one.* Go back down our driveway and almost as soon as you get back on the main boulevard, make a quick cut to your right. You might have to have your car trample over some of the taller weeds to start down her driveway, but I assure you, it is right there."

I shook my head and then nodded. *What had I gotten myself into?* Though I was still committed to meeting Zita, some part of me said it might be best to *run for the hills!* "Thank you," I said, which I then stupidly followed up with, "I don't know how I missed it," - a blatant untruth, as anybody would have missed it! It would have been more appropriate to have said, *"She should have warned me that her driveway was indiscernible from the patches of thicket growing alongside the roadway."*

But then this kind woman made me feel better as I got in my car and started backing out of her driveway. "It's no problem at all, *and you're not alone in that category*. Tell Zita we said hello." And with that, she waved goodbye and stepped back away from the window. I would find out later that this woman and her husband, an elderly couple who had been married for decades, had purchased their portion of this land from Zita and had built that beautiful and modern home there. Part of their routine was to check in on Zita every so often, the kind of neighbors which suited Zita just fine … present when needed, but not intrusive or suffocating.

I pulled the car around and headed out of the driveway, then did as I had been told, made a right and looked to turn right once again into Zita's elusive driveway. *Oh my God!* I thought I saw what once had been a driveway, from decades before, hidden behind wildly thriving bushes that flanked an overgrown patch of weeds, dead branches, shoulder-high grass, thistles, *and who knew what all else might be growing there.* The flora had entirely camouflaged the entrance, making it blend into the side of the road so seamlessly that almost anyone looking for Zita's would only stumble upon her driveway by sheer luck.

I slowed my car to a crawl and turned in hesitantly. As my front fender plowed down the brush, I heard an unfamiliar sound for driving, something more like the scraping one hears when they are shoveling snow off of hard pavement. I immediately came to a small bridge, and once over that, I was past the weeds, and I could now see that I was connected to a long dirt path which ended in a circular clearing where the old, Revolutionary War era house rose into view. Not exactly

The Adamms Family home, but a quite-close, second cousin.

The early spring and an obvious lack of upkeep had taken its toll on the structure and grounds. The home itself was pre-Victorian-style and quite historical: two stories with those wide, pitched windows, sprouting proud, triangular posts out of the roof. I would find out later on it had been built in 1793, and *that much was clear.* To the right of the house was a large garage also suffering from inadequate maintenance, but somehow, it was still standing strong. Behind the garage was one more building, what looked to be a small guest house, also in dire need of repair. In front of the garage and the house, the overgrown lawn was filled with a large assortment of robust weeds and sprawled out in an unsightly manner until it abutted the thick woods occupying the remaining acres of what, I assumed, was the rest of her property. *Perhaps it would be better to just quietly retrace my steps and call it a day ....*

I immediately halted my negative thoughts and focused instead on: *milestone!* I took a deep breath and opened my car door. A large oak tree overlooked the front porch and provided protection from the hot sun. I took the tree's majesty, along with the inviting shade it provided, as a gentle welcome as I ambled towards the front steps.

Clearly, the house had once been a stately property even though this was hard to tell now, and I made my way up the three steps of the large, wrap-around, front porch that was quite weathered and worn. Wood beams stretched the entire length of the house, and colonial pillars rose to connect with the roof. Old, white paint was peeling off in large flakes from everything, and they hung precipitously from almost every area. Two oak rockers sat off to the side of the front door, their broken woven seats showing the wear of lazy summer days gone way by. Although I could picture this Victorian-style house, if painted black and decorated for Halloween, looking like Morticia and Gomez's place; as I got closer to the front door, in the late spring light of a strengthening afternoon sun and with the oak tree as guardian, I was suddenly thinking of another TV family who might be sitting out on the front porch during a late summer evening.

The domicile now reminded me more of the set of *The Waltons,* and I envisioned John-boy out here giving Mary Ellen, Zebulon, and Jim-Bob a lesson about what would happen to their home if proper upkeep lapsed and maintenance went by the wayside. I could hear their voices in my head. *"Stop it, John-boy, you're scaring us!" Mary Ellen would say. "It's for your own good, Mary Ellen,"* John-boy *would answer, giving Jim-Bob's hair a tassel.* "Maybe now you'll both remember to sweep the porch and cut the grass once in a while!"

Despite all of this, I was still pretty excited and confident about meeting Zita. The appearance of the unkempt property had done nothing to assuage my enthusiasm because Hollywood actors were all known for their eccentricities. I took a deep breath and stretched out my hand to press the faded white button of the doorbell. Almost immediately, I heard a *"Hello! Hello!"* Zita appeared at a window above the porch to the right. Her initial puzzled, almost alarmed, look quickly broke into a smile, and she had the same glamor as the night before when she had appeared to me in our living room. "I'll be right down." She vanished from the window, leaving the sheer white curtains to blow gently in the breeze.

Soon, I heard the rustle of the doorknob, and I watched it turn as the door flew open. It was then that I saw Zita clearly for the first time. Standing before me in all of her elegant beauty, I would have sworn she was sixty-two and not seventy-nine years young. Though she was a small figure, her eyes were wide open, and they conveyed a large exuberance of energy, along with a touch of surprise. *For a fleeting instant, I wondered if she remembered who I was and that we had a meeting scheduled today.* Then, as if she was the actress on a film shoot and was portraying a plantation owner calling for her butler in a scene right out of *Gone with the Wind,* Zita swung one arm back and with much gusto, she yelled, *"Brandy and Peanuts!"*

I tilted my head in confusion. *Certainly, we were not going to begin our mentorship chomping on peanuts while sipping brandy out of snifters?* Just then, a large black German shepherd and a wire-haired, white and tan terrier, ran swiftly around Zita's legs. As they made a beeline straight for me, I patted each of them on the head as Zita looked down and shouted at them, *"Brandy, Peanuts, stay!"*

The dogs sat at my feet and that's when Zita extended her hand towards me. I took it within my own. I was immediately reminded of Angela, the elderly actress back at the Elmwood Playhouse who had helped to "motivate" me to try out for the role of chorus boy in *The Boy Friend.* "Zita," I said confidently, as if we were long-lost relatives. "It's so nice to meet you in person. I'm Tom Stratford; we spoke on the phone."

"Yes. It's very nice to meet you, as well. *Tom,* did you say? Yes, come in - come in, Tom. That is your name, right? How do you do?" Her initial look of surprise was gone and was now replaced with some of the assurance I had noticed from her interview the night before.

I took a few steps inside the doorway. "I am fine, thank you. *I am so happy to be here.*"

She stared at me silently and in utter stillness for an uncomfortable moment. *"Are you gay?"* she asked, without hesitation. Though I was floored, I tried to hide my surprise as she continued. "I hope not. *I've had my share of that.*" She turned and took a few steps into the house before briefly looking back at me in an almost accusatory fashion. I stood there, speechless, simply smiling at her. With that, she called Brandy and Peanuts to follow us inside and I had lost the opportunity to respond in any way, because by then, Zita was on the move.

I followed her into the foyer and my eyes scanned the hallway. Ghosts of the past seemed very much alive within the walls of this historical house, which once, *must have been an incredible showplace and entertainment spot for the showbiz crowd.* Now dark and dusty, the interior sported cobwebs in the top corners of the ceiling. I followed Zita into the living room, or parlor as she called it, which was furnished with beautiful, deep-red, oriental carpets and period-appropriate furniture. The couches were rich and luxurious, light blue velvet and very large, with cushions that looked as bouncy as a trampoline bed. There was a grandfather clock, several huge, marble-topped end tables, and the kind of dark wooden bookshelves which had fancy and intricately carved paisley designs at top and all along each of their four supporting poles. The windows looking out into the back garden were almost entirely covered by extendable, thick, dark gray curtains.

The parlor combined with the dining room, making for one large room with several distinct areas. As we walked through the dining area, I saw a large, round, oak dining table which had eight chairs around it, but the chairs and the table were covered in a thin layer of dust and had obviously not welcomed guests in quite some time. Here, heavy, tan, brocade curtains lined the windows and allowed only a few filtered rays of sunlight to shine through. I noticed immediately that part of the table was covered with stacks of what looked to be old headshots of Zita, some dating back as far as 1934. Newspapers and books were scattered over the rest of it, and I wondered just how long ago they had last been touched.

Zita gestured for us to return to the parlor area, where we sat across from one another in velvet chairs. The parlor was cozy and comforting, and yet, I immediately had the uncanny sense that we were not actually alone in the room. My mind became preoccupied feeling the presence of spirits from years past, and I thought, if indeed they were here, *they would enjoy sitting with us and listening in.* "So, Tom," Zita started, breaking my foray into the spiritual plane of existence. "It is very nice to meet you. I do hope you are serious about taking acting lessons. You see, I have been able to get through life because I am always ready."

"Ready?" I questioned. *"How do you mean ready?"*

Zita leaned toward me. "Well, you see my prayers and my strong belief in the Gods have prepared me, and now I am ready…do you see?" She sat up straight in her chair, confident that her message had been quite clear and precise.

I had no exact idea what Zita was actually getting at, but I responded with my first thought. "I do know that prayers are important…"

"Yes! *Yes!*" she cried out. "And that is something that you must study as well, and then as you learn to like it, you, too, will become ready."

I was at a loss for words; her line of thoughts had done nothing but confuse me, so I took my time letting my eyes roam the adjoining rooms. The living room was spacious and obviously rich in history. Zita watched me for a moment and then continued. "Well, let's get to know each other. How is your family? *You do have family here, don't you?*"

Grateful that this was at least a question I knew how to answer, I quickly replied, "Yes. *Yes, I do.* They are doing fine, thanks. And how about you? How's your family?"

"I have a sister," Zita said. She spoke softly but with conviction. "She is in a home now, and I don't get to see her much anymore, *you see?*" I thought I detected a momentary sadness cross her eyes, but she moved the conversation forward. "Now let's see…you said you believed in God?"

"Yes, I do." I made sure that my words were spoken with a firm clarity. Even though I was a little dumbfounded with this entire conversation so far, I was still eager to confirm my role as her obedient student.

"Well, great for you. I have some homework for you, but that's for later. You see, ever since I was young, I have done my homework. And now? *Huh?* What did you say?" Her brows lifted in confusion, but she still kept a bright smile upon her face.

Eager to put her at ease, I quickly said, "No - that wasn't me. I didn't say anything." For a moment, I wondered if one of the spirits listening in on us had perhaps tried to warn her about something.

"Oh, yes. Yes, of course. Let me get the Book of Prayers for you and we will also read Hamlet, so you should get a copy of the play."

Now we were getting somewhere, I thought. *Hamlet would be just the kind of classical drama I needed, having lessons to enact which would be simply great to learn!* Zita rose from her chair and headed to the stairway, climbing steadily toward the second floor. I followed her to the bottom of the steps and squinted my eyes, trying to focus on what I was seeing. The stairs were lined from top to bottom with what looked to be a hundred or so bottles of vitamins and assorted natural herbs. *Maybe that's why she looks so much younger than her age!* I gave a faint nod and lifted my eyebrows, then headed back into the living room.

I found myself beside a cherrywood table which was up against the far wall, and, just like the table in the dining room, it held a stack of *Zita* headshots from long ago. Zita returned down the stairs and came into the living area as I was still admiring her appearances in the headshots. *"Look at these shots,"* I remarked. "You look great. I'd love to have one, *may I?"*

"What would you want one for?" She seemed genuinely puzzled by my request. "That was so long ago and not at all important now. You see, I've been there, and I've come back. Now I'm ready to go on…you see?" She laid the well-worn leather book she had brought down on the table next to the stack of photos.

"Well, yes, I do see. But still, it would be great to have one of them for myself. Could I, and… would you sign it, too?" *I wasn't about to walk away without one of those classical photos.*

"Fine," Zita acquiesced. "What do you want me to write?"

"I don't really know," I answered. "Whatever you'd like."

With a lack of enthusiasm, almost as if I was being a nuisance now, Zita picked-up the black marker at the top of the table and signed her name with a flourish, then handed me the photo. "Okay, let's talk about the lessons. I charge $30.00 per lesson, and I suggest two or three each week."

As much as I was glad that she had moved onto the real reason I was there, I was nervous about the prospect of telling her that I had some strict financial concerns, and that I could not handle that many sessions per week. I looked at her with my best sheepish eyes. "I can understand the benefit of that many lessons," I said, "but honestly, I just can't afford to pay for more than one

session a week." I desperately hoped that agreeing to
only one lesson per week would not be a deal-breaker.

This is the actual photo Zita signed for me.

She wrote: To Tom In Faith Zita Johann

Almost as if she was prepared for and perhaps even expecting my retort, she said, "Well, okay. We can figure something out. We can make some sort of an arrangement. For now, you can just come by tomorrow and write down the prayers I have for you. Can you be here tomorrow?"

I found myself admiring her commanding presence which, in no way, left any room for debate. Without hesitation, I responded. "Yes. I can be here tomorrow after I finish work around 5 o'clock."

"Fine. Then we can work out a schedule, okay?" Without missing a beat, she continued, "You can take me to the market tomorrow and I will give you a free lesson in exchange during the week. *Here come the arrangements.*"

What she had just said about the arrangements coming informed me that she was willing to barter in order to provide me with lessons. *This struck me as both generous and a little unexpected.* I only paused very briefly, since this agreement would serve to help me reach my goals and, for that alone, I was grateful. *Milestone in play.* "Yes, Zita. That will be fine; *I appreciate it.* I will see you tomorrow at five." I extended my hand and she took it.

With that, we shook on it and a deal had been made....

She smiled and nodded, and I did likewise, then turned to make my way to the front door, delicately and carefully cradling her headshot in my left hand. *Zita Johann* was willing to take me on as a student, *and she was serious about it!* I floated out the door and down those weathered steps without giving the disheveled property a second thought. *To hell with John-boy's admonishment!*

As I hopped into my car, pure excitement surged through my veins. *I was about to embark on classical, hands-on training with a famous actress from Hollywood's Golden Era. No matter what else might be thrown my way in the days to come, I was willing to learn whatever Zita Johann wanted to teach me, and I could not wait to return....*

***

Chapter Five

Beginnings & Ends

***

In our first meeting, Zita had definitely captured my interest. I wasn't about to miss a minute of my first lesson, so I arrived at her house promptly at 5 o'clock the following day. This time, I had no trouble finding her driveway. I practically ran up the weathered steps of her home, said hello to Mary Ellen, Zebulon, and Jim-Bob, and eagerly knocked on the door. It didn't take long for Zita to open the door and usher me straight into the parlor. Now familiar with me, Peanuts and Brandy wagged their tails and settled for a pat on the head before returning to their bed on a soft blanket below the window.

Zita began our time together by emphasizing just how important it was to prepare myself with prayer and exercise. "Have a seat on the floor, Tom, it's best you start with a little yoga this afternoon."

I was open to trying anything she might suggest. After all, she was an accomplished actor, and I was committed to following her lead. *If yoga will up my game, then so be it.* My legs crumpled under me as I sat down on the oriental rug directly across from where she was seated comfortably in her chair.

"Now, put your legs straight out in front of you and stretch your body down and out," she directed. "Yoga is so good for your body and your mind."

I followed her instructions and did my best to comply, breathing in and out deeply. Slowly I bent forward and tried unsuccessfully to reach my toes. I wasn't the most flexible person, but I tried my best, feeling a little awkward but also committed to doing what had been asked of me.

"Now lie back and slowly raise your legs up and over your right shoulder, tilting your head in the opposite direction. That's it. Go on, all the way back."

Zita reminded me of a gym teacher I had had a few years back, always pushing students to the limit, never letting anyone slack off. I was using all the strength I could muster to do what she wanted, and I hoped it was going to satisfy her. I braced my back with my hands and gave myself an extra push in order to get my legs to where they were supposed to go. *Yoga. In Zita Johann's parlor.* I kept reminding myself this was serving a purpose and wasn't just *an exercise in humiliation.*

"Legs back down and then up and over your left shoulder, turning your head this time to the right." Her voice never wavered from its firm, but encouraging tone, and I continued to follow her lead.

This Yoga stuff was brand new to me, but after a little bit of time, my body was actually warming up to the exercise. I was surprised to feel relief from tightness and stress in my back as I moved and stretched following her directions. For about thirty minutes, she had me try various positions and poses, all the while reminding me to breathe with focus and intention. Finally, Zita let me know that my first yoga session was officially completed. "That was a good start, Tom. You have some things to practice, but you will get there."

I was relieved to be done with the exercise for the day, but I had to admit to myself that Zita might be on to something. What had started with my initial skepticism had progressed to, not just blind acceptance, but an understanding about how this could affect not only my body but maybe even my mind. *A little bit of yoga, and I felt like I was beginning to soak up some of Zita's Hollywood magic.*

Two more things to note about the exercise routine Zita had introduced me to on that first day. One, stretching my body in that way had such an impact on me and how I felt, that it is something I continue to practice even to this day. On a more humorous note, later on during that first lesson, I thought about my position on the floor, and it being summer and all, I had been wearing shorts. How had that presented itself to Zita as she oversaw my workout from her perch on her chair?

She must have had a clear view of certain parts of my body as I moved my l*egs up and over my shoulder,* following her precise instructions! *Zita ...!*

Once the exercise portion of our meeting was done, I asked to use the bathroom. Zita walked me to a door at the opposite end and underneath the staircase and opened it, flipping the light switch on the wall. "The bathroom is down there," she said, pointing her fingers down the narrow steps to the basement. "Once you get to the bathroom, there is a chain hanging down from the ceiling that will turn on the light." *Okay, so once again, I began thinking of Morticia and Gomez's haunted mansion.*

I started down the narrow wooden stairs, the dim light casting eerie shapes and shadows on the walls. The floorboards squeaked with each step I took, until I finally reached the stone floor at the bottom. The only light was from a tiny bulb in the middle of the ceiling which managed to squeak out just a bit of illumination in the main room. Straight ahead was a wall, so I turned left until I came to another wall where a doorway opened up toward a vast and dim storage space which was practically devoid of any light whatsoever. I looked around for a bathroom door and spotted a tiny hallway off to the left.

As my eyes adjusted to the darkness, I followed that hall beside the storage space, but right before I did so, my eyes caught sight of a shadowy figure on the other side of the doorway I had just passed through. I hurried to the end of this hall, now knowing I needed to speed through my time in the basement, and finally I made out a half-bathroom all the way at the end of the hall. I was now breathing quite rapidly as my hands reached up, hoping to find the chain hanging from the ceiling. Once I felt it, I grasped it tightly and pulled it down, and I immediately welcomed the yellow glow that bathed the small room in light. *Surely, that shadowy figure had just been my imagination.*

Before leaving the bathroom, I steadied my breathing. I tried to keep my eyes focused straight ahead as I made my way back to the stairs leading to the main floor. My ears were pricked up to listen for any sort of noise indicating movement. I was relieved when I saw the light from the lone bulb in the main room, and then the staircase just to the right. *However, I then found myself not being able to resist the temptation to take one last look back.* I glanced over my shoulder, and I immediately felt the energy and existence of another soul. In that instant, I was confident it was the presence of *a Revolutionary War soldier.*

Perhaps my childhood spent in a home built by my grandfather during the Great Depression in 1934 is responsible, at least in part, to my familiarity with the spiritual world. As crazy as this may sound, I knew that what I had seen and felt in Zita's basement that evening was real as sure as these words on this page. My childhood home had a large center hall, a design named for this unique style, and it was one of the first of its kind in that area. We entertained friends and family there for many years and even as a young child, I was somehow aware that the house was packed from the basement to the attic with spiritual energy. I felt it constantly, and so my experience at Zita's didn't really alarm me, although at first, it had taken me by surprise.

Once I had made my way back into the living room, I took a few moments to gather my senses as I tried to process what I had seen and felt. I walked around the living room, enjoying the breeze that wafted through the large open windows and reading titles of books in the bookcase. It was fun to imagine living in upstate New York in this peaceful, spacious home, entertaining some of the Manhattan set during the 1940's. *I could only imagine who might have attended some of Zita's parties over the decades. The house and grounds must have been spectacular back then* ... and then my eye spotted a giant and wispy cobweb in the corner of the ceiling, and I immediately snapped out of my reverie. My thoughts moved on to wondering how long it had been there and what, *pray tell,* might have been responsible for its creation. For sure, I didn't want to point it out to Zita for fear of being asked to get it down. As you probably have figured out by now: *I don't like spiders ... and I'm not too big a fan of snakes either.*

A few seconds later, Zita came down the stairway and I made my way to join her. She had *Hamlet* in tow, along with another book. "Now, I thought it would be delightful to start by reading *Hamlet.*" She eagerly thrust the *other* book towards me. "This one," she said, tapping the cover emphatically with two fingers, "is the book I wrote - the one I discussed on *The Joe Franklin Show,* entitled *After the End.* You did see me on TV that night, didn't you?" she asked, almost accusingly.

"Of course, Zita - my mom and I loved it. You were fabulous!"

She looked at me suspiciously, but then that quickly turned into a look of feeling honored. "Yes, well, I rather thought he had rushed me somewhat through my answers, but all went well. Your mom enjoyed the show?" I nodded enthusiastically, and then she smiled and returned her attention to the two books. "We will be using the screenplay to the book as lessons as we go on, so you must read the entire book beforehand."

"Of course, Zita," I replied. "I am honored to be reading your book." *And really, I was genuinely honored to be trusted with it.*

"But, be very careful with it," Zita emphasized. "*Do not,* under any circumstances, let that book out of your sight! It's the only copy I have, and I only have one copy of the screenplay as well, but we will get to that later on."

I tucked the book carefully under my arm, as if a valuable treasure. "I'll be careful, Zita. I can't wait to get started with reading it." We had been in the parlor, and I mistakenly glanced up at the ceiling to make sure the spider whose web I had observed had not decided to come out to entertain the new guest of the house.

Zita caught my distraction, but thankfully, she had misinterpreted it. "You like my house, *do you, Tom?*"

Relieved, I nodded vigorously. "It is just amazing to me, Zita!"

"Yes, well, it has good bones, as they say. It was built in 1793; a true Revolutionary War Era home."

I shook my head in amazement and put my hands on my hips, jutting a smile outward to her as I told myself that over-gesticulating was usually taken as a sign of approval by Zita. "Wow - what a history it must have."

She smiled and continued. "I purchased it in 1938, and moved in during 1939, when the house was already nearly a hundred-and-fifty years old."

That was certainly plenty of time to become chock full of supernatural energy, so seeing a

Revolutionary War soldier would have been quite appropriate for the time period. "These walls must have seen so much over the years," I said, thinking to myself that perhaps the figure and the energy I had felt down in the basement had come to me portending a good omen as to my mentorship with Zita.

"Yes, well so have I," she responded, not missing a beat. Before I could say anything else, she continued, "For now, we will start with *Hamlet.*" Zita sat down comfortably in the living room, and I took my seat across from her as well. The pair of chairs were covered in lush velvet and quite comfortable. I sank back into the cushions and opened *Hamlet.* For the next hour I read scenes to Zita, and she seemed to take great delight in offering suggestions and corrections. I loved the immediate feedback and did my best to follow through on her directions.

Zita had me repeat certain lines over and over again, asking me to read them with different emotions, and this contributed to an exercise in using precise vocal pitch, volume, and rhythm. I was amazed as I noticed how small changes in my voice and in my delivery could alter the meaning behind the words I read. I had actually never read *Hamlet* before, and I had little understanding of the story when we began. As I read it more thoroughly, I was able to embody some of the precise characteristics of the roles, and I began speaking lines with greater meaning because I began to understand the various nuances to each of the characters.

When this first lesson was over, I believed that I had stumbled upon a great find with having Zita as my acting coach. I just knew, more than ever, that she was going to help me to expand my repertoire of acting skills. As I got into my car after that first full lesson, I was eager to get home and bury my nose in her book, mostly because I was beginning to have so many questions regarding her life, Hollywood, and the theater. She had charmed me not just with her expertise, but also with a personality, which was both quirky and mysterious. I found myself fascinated thinking about all that she had gone through in her life to get where she was now. I wanted to know more about her life story, and for now, reading her book seemed to be a good way to get started learning something new about her.

When I returned to Zita's house for my next session, I was full of questions. She opened the door and led me once again into the living room. Each session would begin with thirty minutes of stretching exercises and would be my new routine, and I thought that might be a good time to get Zita talking about her past.

151

As I lifted my legs up and over my head from my prone position on my back just a few feet away from where she was sitting in her Queen Anne chair, I said, "Zita, I'd love to hear what it was like for you in Hollywood during the 1930's." I glanced between my legs in her direction enough to know she had heard me, but when I saw that she was taking a distinct interest in fluffing the pillow in her chair, I knew that she was sending me the message that she wasn't about to entertain my questions. I wanted to know so much about what it was like being in Hollywood during the 1930s, but I was beginning to understand that she was not fond of reminiscing. Disappointed, I put my legs back in front of me with my feet on the floor and began shifting them left and right. It was difficult for me to understand why Zita was reluctant to talk about her past.

When she was satisfied that I was sufficiently warmed up, she motioned for me to return to my chair. "Let's start with scene 3 in *Hamlet* today," she instructed. Our second lesson was just as informative as the first, and as I grew accustomed to reading Hamlet, I began feeling better about my understanding of its complexities. In fact, even today, when I think about some of my favorite plays of all time, *Hamlet* always makes the list. That is likely due to the combination of Shakespeare's great writing along with the fact that I cherished the attention to detail Zita gave to my performance - and truly, our entire mentorship, right from the start of working with her.

And so, this second lesson proceeded with a confident report - there were verbal exercises, facial expressions, emotive training, and gesturing on cue. Zita liked the repetitive nature of the lessons in that she knew the more I practiced the same routine, the more it would become second-nature to me. I followed without argument, and found that within her presence, a new sort of confidence began to resonate within me. At the end of our second session, when it was time for her to escort me to the front door, instead I saw Zita relax back into her chair. I decided to remain seated and wait patiently to see what was to come.

"Sometimes, I don't like thinking about the past. How I ever made it out there in that degenerate town is beyond me. Let me give you a little history."

I didn't want to look as overjoyed as I felt, so I gave Zita a gentle smile and nod of my head, then settled into my chair to listen.

Her face became blank for just a moment as she considered where to start, and then she looked into my eyes, and I immediately became transfixed by her stare.

"I was born in Timisoara, Romania in 1904, and when I was six, my family moved to America. We settled in Pennsylvania for a short while and then made a home for ourselves in Manhattan at 401 East 58th Street." (*Interesting fun fact: a few years later, when I moved into New York City, I lived at 401 East 62nd Street*).

She eyed me carefully to make sure she had my complete and undivided attention, which of course, she did. "I took an early interest in theater, and at eighteen was enrolled in a school for theater arts and that is when I had my first audition." Zita shook her head in amusement at the memory. "The Theater Guild was looking to hire extra performers for their upcoming season. The pay was thirty-five dollars a week, which seemed fine to me as a start."

I chanced upon a question. "Were you nervous at your first audition, Zita?"

"So nervous that when I finished my audition, I practically ran out of that room!" Zita chuckled softly as she answered and then continued her story. "But lucky for me, Basil Sydney, the producer and director of The Theater Guild, was impressed with my reading. Before I could make my escape through the doors, he asked me to come back."

"Wow - how fascinating! What was running through your mind when he asked you to come back?" I asked.

"Excitement, nervousness, dread, but also anticipation somewhere in the back of my mind that perhaps I had made a quite good first impression. I am sure I hung my head as I headed back toward him, but he was quick to sense my confusion and promptly set things straight. *He asked me if I'd be interested in reading for one of the leads!*"

"That must have been such a shock to you!" I smiled and then noticed how Zita's eyes twinkled with delight as she had recalled this first significant achievement.

"Of course, I was eager to read for him again once I understood what was happening. I put all of my energy into that second reading - I gave it all I had, as they say. Well, Tom, let me tell you, I broke out into a wide smile when Basil told me that I had just landed my first lead role. *In no time at all* I had gone from having the potential of making thirty-five dollars a week to the certainty of earning a hundred dollars a week as a leading lady for the Theater Guild's 1922 season. *Imagine that!*"

I shook my head, grinning broadly in admiration as I leaned in closer to Zita. "What an auspicious beginning, Zita! How fortunate for you that everything fell into place on your very first audition!"

Now that Zita had gotten started telling me stories about her life, she seemed genuinely happy to be doing so. I focused solely on her, watching her eyes light up as she recalled specific and rather significant things which had happened so long ago. I kept telling myself that this was an education well beyond anything I could ever learn on the stage itself, or from a book. And I was beginning to understand that although Zita was hesitant to talk much about herself, once she got going, she could continue at length in an entertaining stream of memories from one subject right into another.

"Believe it or not," she said to me as if we were just like old friends reminiscing in front of a fire, and I now felt I had earned that possibility and honor of potentially sharing snifters of Brandy with Zita.

Speaking of which, I glanced towards the front door and was comforted by the sight of the two pups lying beside one another, sleeping peacefully on their blanket, content that their mother was enjoying her time with a new friend. "In two years' time," Zita continued, "I had performed in three shows. And then, just guess, Tom, where I landed next?"

"I don't know for sure, Zita, but I am going to say, it seems likely that appearing on Broadway was in your immediate future." I cocked my head to the side, anticipating her response.

"It was," Zita affirmed. "I managed to earn the lead role in a play called *Man and the Masses* first. And then from there, I was constantly landing roles in shows both on and off Broadway." What she said next caught me by surprise and reminded me just how talented Zita truly had been. She said this as an afterthought, not even

aware of how astonishing this would hit me. "I was quite fortunate during those times, and I was able to work with Clark Gable, Edward G Robinson, Alfred Lunt, and Lyn Fontanne, among many others. Most of them were rather unknown at the time."

I shook my head, absolutely amazed. "Zita, you experienced so much success right from the start. Your career really took off - I can only imagine what it was like knowing you had acted with such greats so early in your beginnings."

She crossed one leg over the other and jiggled her foot up and down, and I wondered if I had made a gaffe. Of course, I considered her as great as any of them, but I realized this may not have come through in my word choice. I did not want to make it worse and so I kept silent. I then did a quick glance to the ceiling, checking for that creepy spider, and was happy when I did not see it. "To be honest, I seemed to be in demand," she continued, choosing not to address those more famous actors, and I felt relieved. "There were national tours that always included shows in Los Angeles - *Hollywood* to be exact." The way she said the word *Hollywood* was as if spitting it out of her mouth with great distaste. "After my performance out there in a show called *Machinal*, *Hollywood* directors and producers began contacting me almost immediately."

Now we were on to the good stuff, I thought to myself, and my hands gripped the edges of both armrests.

Zita offered a slight laugh but then hung her head for a moment. "It was during *Machinal,* that I met John Houseman who was, at the time, a theatrical producer." She paused and her eyes became misty, not quite teary, but I could tell some part of this recollection brought her a bit of pain. "Well, we started spending a lot of time together and as you can imagine, romance blossomed. At that same time, I was offered a contract with MGM, and I started to think about moving to Hollywood permanently."

She paused just for a moment, but long enough for me to respond. "That would have been a big move for anybody. Were you nervous at all when you thought about making such a life-changing move?"

"Truthfully, the deal was just too good to pass up. Mr. Thalberg, the studio executive at MGM who had offered me the contract, included in it the clause that I was to have final script approval. So, I would have been crazy to hesitate." Zita leaned back in her chair and her eyes took on a distant look for a moment. "You know, Tom, back in those days, it just wasn't safe for a young lady to be traveling across the country alone. My mother

offered to come to Hollywood with me, and this was the safest thing to do back then. Well, I agreed, and we made the move."

"If my memory serves me well, this still would have been about the time that talking motion pictures were just starting to become popular?" *I had hoped I was correct; otherwise, be made to look unknowledgeable about my own industry.*

"Yes!" I nodded and silently let out a breath of relief. "Because of that," Zita continued, "searching for just the right voice to supplement great acting for those to be chosen for roles in their movies was of paramount importance to casting directors." She paused and looked towards the window by the front door, and when she spoke next, I was certain there was more than a hint of regret in her tone. "It seemed that not only did I have some talent, but I had a voice which many directors found to be just what they wanted."

I nodded affirmatively, and then cocked my head to the side and looked at her closely. Her lack of enthusiasm was not what I had expected as she reported this quite favorable turn of events in her history. "Zita - I'm sensing that something may not have gone the way you had hoped it would." Although I felt a sudden sadness descend upon the room, I was honestly still thrilled that Zita felt close enough to me that she could share such personal information.

"Well … within a short amount of time, I was given three roles to review, *none of which suited me. There were three directors I was to work with, and I didn't want to work with any one of them."* Now Zita was in her element - completely enlivened with a show of her stubborn side, which she never relinquished just to foster her own popularity. It was clear to me that she would never even consider to compromise on the value of the projects she chose. "I was given script after script to review, and they were garbage. I did not like any of them, and since I had the right to refuse, *I did just that!* They still had to pay me under the terms of the contract I had signed."

And now she smiled in such a way that she was instantly glamorous once again. "Six months after having moved out to *Hollywood*, we packed our bags, I bid Mr. Thalberg a respectful goodbye, *and we returned to New York twenty-seven thousand dollars richer.*"

Shaking my head in wonder, I managed to say, "You are something, Zita - that's for certain!"

She gave me her best seductive smile, and I imagined her holding one of those long cigarette holders that all of the actresses back in those days used as a prop, letting it dangle just so precariously from her fingertips, as she blew a long plume of white smoke towards me.

"Well, you see, Tom, I was very eager to get back to my theater roots, and also … I knew I was ready to marry John Houseman."

It was getting late, and I could tell she was very tired. I decided not to ask about her marriage at this time. I was certain that there would be other opportunities to do so yet to come. Standing from my chair, I said, "This is all so fascinating to me, Zita, and I am so appreciative that you felt like you could share it with me." I gave her my warmest smile and the awe I felt for her had grown considerably. *Zita was a force to be reckoned with - she had taken on Hollywood at a young age on her own terms and navigated the circumstances to suit herself.*

Zita stood from her chair, and I wanted to embrace her as I would my own grandmother, but I held back. Instead, I simply said, "Thank you, Zita, for the lessons *and for telling me some things about your incredible past.* I'll see you next week for our next session."

I turned towards the front door, ecstatic about what I had just learned. I couldn't wait to tell my mom - again, I felt that this was just the kind of education one cannot acquire by any means except for hearing it from the person who had actually lived it! How many actors today would pass up *any roles they had been offered* when they were trying to first bust into the industry?

That night, I read almost her entire novel, *After the End.* My first impression was how brilliant is this? *It needed to get published!* Coupled with the opportunity to read the screenplay of her novel with Zita herself was a great experience. She was constantly helping me to understand what was expected when reading directly from a screenplay, which was not written out as extensively as a novel would be. As far as character development, Zita would continuously ask me questions meant to help me to define my character and his intentions.

We would spend weeks reading both from her screenplay and from *Hamlet*, and having done so, *we would then begin to plan other lessons ... other adventures together.*

***

Chapter Six

The Starlight Shines but for Pizza and Cookies

***

My lessons with Zita took on their own routines, which included spending time with Zita away from reading Hamlet as well as the book that Zita herself had written, *After the End.* I had made it clear to Zita that I could only afford one lesson a week, and so she had graciously devised a plan which would make it possible for me to work with her more often. Once a week, as her chosen method of payment for a second/extra lesson for that week, I would drive her to run errands. Sometimes this would mean a trip to the post office and grocery store, and other times it might be to the beauty parlor or to her lawyer's office. It never mattered to me where she needed me to take her since I was happy to be helping her in this way, and the payoff for me was the benefit of another lesson under my belt.

As I spent more time with Zita over the coming months, I would come to learn that her approach to the occult and to prayer were practically one and the same and were practices she had developed early on in her life. Long before moving into this house, Zita had made friends with the spiritual world through her practice of praying to the gods - gods of wealth, or power, or health, *or whatever might be needed at the time.* In different ways, each of us had developed a connection to the spiritual world; for me it was sensing the spiritual energy which lived in the house where I had been raised, and for

Zita, it was her belief in the power of her prayers to various Gods. That she prayed to various Gods did not bother me at all, because I figured she had come this far with her beliefs, and they had served her well. Although I didn't recognize it as such at the time, looking back, I believe we both had a common thread of faith - each of us elicited our higher powers for our own personal needs.

As our lessons in the living room parlor continued further into the summer, I was becoming well-versed in my understanding of *Hamlet* and thrilled that we were continuing with readings from the screenplay version of her book. After having devoured the novel version of *After the End*, I found it to be brilliant, and having the chance to read the screenplay with her was quite amazing. Zita's story centered around twelve men and women who found themselves seeking shelter in the form of a hotel lounge with an adjoining diner. Little by little, these men and women realize that they are no longer among the living, and they are tasked with trying to discover what had led them to this hotel lounge rather than ascending directly to their "final destination" of heaven. In order to do so, each of them must battle beyond a tough situation they had faced during their lives in order to find the peace and understanding necessary to move forward in the afterlife.

Once any of the twelve finally come to accept a new and functional manner of dealing with whatever it was in life which had brought them to their specific impasse, they would then make their ascent. In Zita's story, the ascent comes by way of Michael, who chauffeurs a limo and comes in the middle of the night to pick-up the lucky ones who have figured out what was necessary, and then he drives them to their final destination.

I have to say that back in the mid-1980's, this

concept was quite original, although since then, any

number of movies and television series have tackled

similar subject matter. Perhaps Zita had been among the

first to write such a treatise about the live-action

struggles of people who have passed and find themselves

stuck in some kind of afterlife limbo. In the pages to

follow, my hope is that my readers will find out why it is

quite possible Zita had been responsible for originating

and promoting this specific means of handling material

of this kind, which has grown to be very popular

recently.

We spent a good deal of time reading from the

After the End script. I was so impressed with how people

came and went by Michael that I wanted to read his part,

But Zita had me read the lead part of Richard first

because he had more interactions, and she wanted me to

focus on the importance of a lead role. Later, we would read other parts that formed supporting roles and Zita elucidated her reasoning by saying that reading the roles of various characters would help me to further develop and broaden my skills, since I would have to transform into different and completely unique roles. I had immediately thought of Travolta and how many roles of such diversity he had taken since his *Vinnie Barbarino* days. *"This method will also help you to see the story from different viewpoints, something that is quite important. Do you see what I mean, Tom?"* Zita had explained.

Reading from Zita's screenplay, I realized this was the very first time that I had held an actual movie script in my hands. Early on in my training, when we read from *After the End*, we had read from several pages of photocopies of various scenes from the actual screenplay. But now that we were into it so deeply, we had begun using the entire script itself. Handling this and realizing it had been written by my acting coach herself, was a special thrill for me. *I cradled those pages like they were gold.* Holding that script tenderly in my hands somehow brought me a special connection right to the depths of Hollywood itself. This had, by far, become my favorite material to read, and as we went on, I began to understand the storyline in all of its intricate detail.

One afternoon, I finally asked Zita the question that had been burning in my mind. I wanted to know more about the process she had undertaken both to get her manuscript published and to get the movie made. To me, it was a great story with such unpredictable characters, and I could not understand why she had not been able to publish it. Also, I felt ripe for auditioning for the main character of Richard once the movie version of her book came to the big screen. "Zita, when do you think this book will get published?"

She huffed out a long plume of exasperated air. "They're all dead, Tom."

The characters? Yes, of course, I knew this already. *But what did that have to do with the book getting published?* I felt stymied, and Zita saw the look of confusion on my face.

"My former producers, directors, and all the other actors I had been able to befriend over the decades - they're all dead now, *and that is why I will not get After the End published at this time.*" I watched Brandy walk over and sit on the carpet between us to scratch his right ear. I had no response.

"You see, Tom - I have nobody left in the industry, and even my agent himself is no longer among the living."

"I am so sorry to hear that, Zita," I finally summoned.

"Yes, all very well, Tom," she responded, and then she cleared her throat.

As I watched her, she began shaking her head rather convincingly. Once she stopped, she looked directly into my eyes. "Remember I told you this: *it's not about how good your manuscript is nowadays, but who you know in the industry who can pitch it to the right people.*"

I nodded solemnly and thought, *but surely there were other ways and means to get your novel into the appropriate hands.*

As if she was reading my mind and knew I was about to pursue my line of thoughts, she changed the subject. "Going to be hot out there today, don't you know?"

And with that I said, *"Yes, Zita it is,"* and believed it best for me to not pursue my line of reasoning at the time.

As our relationship deepened, I came to realize that Zita was adept at making it clear just how important it was to develop a deep sense of someone's character when playing their part - just as it had been for her when writing about them. More importantly, she was able to teach me how crucial it was to develop a character's personality traits through the use of their spoken words. Many of our lessons revolved around the specific trade tips and tools regarding how to use both vocal inflections and facial expressions to nail down the character one was portraying. When done correctly, an actor's performance would then speak volumes to his or her audience about who the character truly was and what they were all about. I knew right away how important and true these specific lessons of Zita's were. Learning to craft a character utilizing these traits, though seemingly minor at first, *truly brought the character to life!*

However, by the end of June, my thoughts turned away from my lessons and towards the annual trip I made each year with my friends to Cape Cod to celebrate July 4th. I was looking forward to driving my friends in my newly acquired 1978 sporty *Firebird.* This classic car suited my persona of being hip and cool, and because my work with Zita had filled me with a renewed sense of confidence that my career in acting was bonafide, I was even more excited to be the one driving and *in charge* of this trip. Once on the Cape, we would always meet up and hang out with eight of our close friends for four days of nonstop fun. There would be relaxing afternoons spent on the beach or at the poolside, our young bodies absorbing the affirming energy of the sun.

But, oh, those hot summer nights ....

The Cape would always be crowded with eager and available singles over the long Fourth of July weekend, and meeting new people provided us with an exciting source of entertainment. Our evenings usually included drinking a little too much in a crowded bar while surrounded by loud music and other young adults looking to party. And then, of course, the highlights which topped off the exuberance of the four-day excursion were watching the seemingly endless displays of the best fireworks out over the ocean, and then spending the remainder of the night wandering between extremely lively Fourth of July parties at a variety of the nicest homes on the Cape.

Of course, the fun eventually had to come to an end, and returning to our "real" lives, jobs, and responsibilities could be quite depressing. The dreaded drive home seemed to always take forever. Since I was the designated driver on this particular trip home, I stopped often to shake off the lethargy and to rejuvenate myself with a cold soda or candy bar. For the first two stops, I climbed out of the car and wandered inside the gas station, but my friends stayed hunched over in their seats, mostly dead to the world. However, the third time I stopped, I realized that my strategy was annoying my friends, who only wanted to nap away the entire trip home, and who preferred the momentum of the highway rather than the parking, stopping, car doors opening and closing, of each of my rest stops.

"You aren't stopping again, are you?" The question was posed by one of my friends, with the others moaning and groaning in agreement.

"Yes, I am," I said. "Unlike you guys, *I have to stay alert on this trip.*"

"We just want to sleep! Don't slam the door!" came the whiny replies. I paid them no attention and headed into the rest area anticipating another hot coffee - after all, I was in charge simply belonging to the fact *that we were in my car* and my being able to drive responsibly would be required to get us safely home. *My sanity was of utmost importance!* Eventually, after a few more stops, we made it home, but admittedly it wasn't done in record time! In fact, that would be the very last time that my friends allowed me to be the driver for our trip.

When I returned home, I had to immediately face unsettling news which my parents had decided to keep from me during my four days of merriment. My beloved grandmother, Antoinette, had passed away. This was extremely difficult for me to bear so suddenly. She had always been important to me - and to my family, *she was our matriarch.* Her life story had been such an inspiration to me throughout my later childhood into my adult years.

At the age of sixteen, during the late eighteen-hundreds, she left her home in Italy and made her way to the United States. In New York City, she soon fell in love, married a good man, and together they started a beautiful family. She became a happy and successful homemaker with seven children, a plethora of grandchildren, and eventually many great-grandchildren. Everyone loved her and spoke highly of her, and she had touched so many lives. Almost everyone in my family cherished their memories involving something Grandma Antoinette had taught them, wisdom she had imparted, or events she had shared with them. She was a great woman with a spirit like no other, and I knew I would miss her dearly.

As for me, to this day, the scent of vine-ripened tomatoes and fresh basil remind me of so many happy summer days spent with Nana picking fresh vegetables from her garden and then watching her prepare a delicious meal in the kitchen. "Always add salt to the water before putting in the pasta, Thomas, it'll cook faster and it won't stick, *and never add oil to the water!*" She would advise me, and I would nod my head and smile up at her, whereupon she would smile back and then wink at me with either one of her beautiful and soulful eyes.

I was finding it was becoming a tough summer to endure, but I soon returned to my lessons with Zita, eager for our mentorship to continue. In all honesty, I was feeling a little bereft due to the loss of my Nana. Part of me felt that being with Zita would be comforting, and I realized that she had inadvertently begun to fill the role of grandmother for me since she was always full of firm direction and encouragement, sort of like a great cheerleader - like most grandparents would be.

On my first return since my vacation, Zita needed to go to the post office right away, and it was during this outing that I found the courage to let Zita know about my grandmother. "I haven't been myself, Zita. My grandmother passed away while I was on vacation."

Zita turned her head in my direction and with softness responded, "Oh, Tom. I am so sorry to hear that. I am sure you must feel just awful." Zita patted my arm gently.

"It was really quite a shock. She was always so full of life and love." I glanced over at Zita and caught her eye for a moment. She nodded thoughtfully, and then there was an uncomfortable silence between us.

I wasn't sure how she would respond to my sharing with her what I was truly feeling at that moment, but I knew what I felt was important to me, and I was compelled to tell her. "Zita, many times when I am with you, I feel like you are just like a grandmother to me - looking out for me the way you do and being so concerned that I learn everything I need to in order to make me the best and most successful actor I can be. I want you to know that I appreciate that, and that I greatly appreciate you."

"What a nice thing to say, Tom. I am going to take that as a genuine compliment! Thank you." Though she might have denied it if asked, I noticed a small smile form on Zita's face, and I had the feeling that it had been a long while since anyone had last given Zita a compliment.

Soon I pulled over to the side of the street, parked beside the post office, and watched Zita enter the small brick building. Our errands together had certainly become part of our routine, and I generally didn't mind them at all. I was already taking her to the supermarket and the post office, the beauty parlor, and periodically to her lawyers, and all this entitled me to free lessons and for that I was grateful. However, when I thought about it at other times, I did worry because, gradually, I was becoming more deeply involved with helping take care of her everyday needs. *What could this lead to?*

It never bothered me if others might think this seemed like a strange arrangement, and for now, it seemed to me to be working just fine. It was always entertaining to be with her, even when we were just running errands. Today would be no different.

Zita opened my car door and climbed back into the front seat. I had been wanting to give her a rundown of where my head was at in terms of my acting career and so I went right into it. "I've been thinking, Zita," I said. "I think I'd like to get involved with some background work in movies and television. Maybe that's how I can make my way to Hollywood."

Instead of her jubilation over my ambitious plans that I had been expecting, Zita became silent, and a pained look flashed across her face. Finally, she countered, "But, Tom, why do you want to get there so fast? *It's not your time yet.* Think about the travel involved. If you are in a show, you will have to tour the country. Are you ready for that? Wouldn't you mind that much traveling?"

I pulled out onto the road to make the slow and relaxing trip back to Zita's. "I wouldn't mind that," I answered. "In fact, I kind of look forward to that part of the process."

"That's good," Zita said. "Because you always have to be ready, like me, I have always been ready to travel on." And then it seemed I hit upon something inside of Zita which could not be stopped! She continued, "It will always be important for you to take care of yourself when traveling and do all you can to keep out of harm's way. That's why prayer is so important, do you understand, Tom? Do you see? I have traveled a lot in my time, from New York to Los Angeles, and many places in between, like Chicago."

We were on the main avenue before we would turn onto Zita's road, and this street had many traffic lights. We were stopped waiting for the green lights just as much as we were actually moving. Turning the volume on the radio down all the way, I said, "I think that would be very exciting for me to experience, as well, Zita."

Zita looked over at me and raised her eyebrow.

"Just for instance, allow me to tell you about this one time when I was in Chicago touring with the play *Uncle Vanya*. I was in my hotel room when the phone rang. I reached over, picked it up, and said, *Hello?* A moment later, a man's voice crackled through the earpiece."

Zita deepened her voice to that of a man in order to represent the person on the other end of the line. *"Miss Zita?"*

And then, back to her own voice, *"Yes,"* and then back and forth from there.

"Al Capone here. I have a problem, and I'm hoping that you can help me out."

"I remained silent for a moment, thinking to myself, *he was hoping I would be over the moon to hear from him,* which I can assure you, Tom, without a doubt, *I certainly was not.* But he continued anyway, completely ignoring my silence."

"If I offered you one hundred dollars, would you go out with me tonight?"

She looked over at me to make sure she had captured my complete and undivided attention. *Which she had!* I interrupted her story, asking, *"Zita! What did you say?"*

"Well, Tom. The moment he had finished asking me his question, I did not hesitate in the slightest. I answered emphatically, *absolutely not! Never!* And with that, Tom, the phone connection clicked dead. Never would I have gone out with him for any reason, and especially not when he'd offered me money. *The nerve of him ... besides, I was a happily married woman at the time!"*

Even though it was a half-century later, Zita's indignation was plain to see. I could almost see the bullets flying out of her eyes as she thought of him, and I would have hated to have been Capone should Zita have crossed paths with him after that. As I watched her expression soften to a playful smile, I fell in love with her at that moment simply due to the firmness of her convictions - and this was just one of the things I admired so much about her.

Other trips into town almost always included insights into Zita's personality, sometimes through humorous moments, and other times by events which mystified me completely. One such trip started out with a short stop at the post office and then a quick run into the vitamin shoppe. Finally, we made our way to the grocery store, and here I climbed out of my car and entered the store with Zita. Slowly, I pushed the cart down the aisles, interested in seeing what Zita would purchase for her own sustenance. Well, when we got to the frozen food section, she hesitated, uncertain what she would need, or want. We were standing right in front of the frozen pizza section, and I thought that would be something good for her to have on hand.

"Zita, why don't you get a few frozen pizzas," I said. "You can keep them in the freezer and then just heat them up in no time."

"What?" Zita raised her chin toward me.

I assumed, at first, that she just hadn't heard me, so I repeated myself. "*A frozen pizza.* Why don't you get a few of those?"

"What is it called?" Her voice held steady, as did her eyes, which were still focused on me, but she raised her eyebrows inquisitively.

"Pizza. Frozen pizza." By this time, I was feeling pretty confused. *Surely, she knew what pizza was?*

She then turned to face me squarely and her arms swung outwards, like angel's wings, her hands splayed outwards and finally came to rest beside her shoulders in a grand gesture of expressing her naivete. She pronounced loudly at the very same time, *"PIZZA?"* as she looked at me with a frown. The tone of her voice had lifted slightly, into that of a question, and at that moment, I was convinced she really had never heard of pizza before. For the life of me, I could not understand how this was even remotely possible.

Glancing around, I realized she had just used her stage voice and theatrical gestures, and the effect had caught the attention of everyone within ear, or eye, shot. Passing shoppers, and anyone else around us (and there were many as it was quite busy), were now shooting glances her way, looking at her strangely, as if she had just washed ashore from the sinking Titanic. With the cart in one hand and taking her arm in the other, I hurried us down the aisle because I was feeling embarrassed by her outburst. We went straight to the register, and I decided to pretend that I hadn't even heard her last exclamation. Looking back on it, though, I still don't really know if she was actually confused, or if maybe she had been toying with me all along, *and everyone else around us at the time for that matter.* Perhaps Zita missed the stage, and she was giving us all a performance, and this was her best version of *Street Theater.*

Well, the fun didn't stop there. As we were heading back to Zita's house, she pulled a package of Stella D'oro cookies out of one of the grocery bags. It happened to be one of my favorites, the assorted collection. She ripped open the bag and offered me a few of the tasty sugar cookies, which I eagerly accepted. Zita plopped the opened bag on the dashboard between the two of us as we continued on toward home. But then, as I made a sharp left turn, the cookies took a sharp right turn directly off the dashboard. As the cookies plunged downward, Zita went to catch them, and at the same moment, she let out a scream so loud and piercing that it temporarily deafened me. Her shrill scream was pitch-perfect, and it sounded much like the scream that made her famous in *The Mummy*; however, it startled me so much that I quickly pulled over. As I watched Zita's reaction, still trying to unsuccessfully catch the cookies, by now they had all, rather unceremoniously, ended up all over the floor of my car.

"Did you see that?" she cackled. "The cookies went all over; *how funny was that?!* But it's okay now."

She reached down to the floor and picked up the bag and all of the cookies which had fallen out. "Okay. I've got them all. We can go now."

My heart skipped a beat. Once again, I was a little confused by her dramatic outburst, this part of Zita was all new to me. I finally accepted it as just one other side to her complicated personality and I pulled back onto the road. Two minutes later, Zita was eating cookies again and she offered me another. All of these were ones which had hit the floor. "No, thank you, I'm good," I said, keeping my eyes on the road and shaking my head imperceptibly in order to release my residual bewilderment.

Turning into the driveway that afternoon, it was difficult for me to overlook the lack of upkeep to the house and property. In many ways since my first visit to Zita's house, I had learned to ignore what was right in front of my eyes: the overgrown bushes, grass, and weeds of the front yard which "welcomed" guests when they first came to see Zita, and the paint peeling from off the wooden beams of the porch. This day, however, I took full note of these conditions, and I was suddenly struck with a feeling of how the house and yard were uncared for, *sort of like Zita herself,* and this then led me to consider how people's situations, as with their things, can certainly change dramatically over time.

Since I liked picturing Zita in her heyday, riding the waves of success with adoring fans and a bright future ahead, it was difficult for me to marry that image with the woman who had just twice screamed bloody murder over something called *pizza* in the frozen food section of a crowded grocery store and falling sugar cookies in a moving car. Now staring at this unkempt

198

residence of hers before me, part of my illusion of who Zita was began to feel a bit threatened.

I parked close to the garage to make it easier to bring groceries through the back door into the kitchen and I helped her put the items away. She seemed methodical and made sure that everything was put into its proper place in the cabinets, the refrigerator, and along the shelves above the sink. She tossed a few treats to Brandy and Peanuts, and then we made our way into the parlor once again, as if nothing odd had ever occurred earlier, and as if nothing between us had changed in the slightest. *It was time to move onto my next lesson.*

***

Chapter Seven

Matinee Idol

***

Things continued as they had been going over the

next several months. Fall had arrived and leaves covered

the yard, and the ones still on the trees all around Zita's

house now seemed painted in quite spectacular displays

of orange, purple, and pink. One afternoon as she

returned from a bathroom break, Zita caught me looking

over some of the framed photos in the hallway of her

with various actors from long before. I wondered if she

could tell that I had been thinking to myself *just what*

had become of any and all of her love interests over the decades? She did not say anything, and of course, I wanted to ask about each of them, but her penchant for privacy outweighed my curiosity, *for now.*

And then, two lessons after, nearing the end of our regular time together, Zita had a surprise for me. "I want you to meet another of my students - a wonderful actress by the name of Lisa. I think the two of you would read well together, and it will be good practice reading with another actor within the same scene."

I was surprised and pleased to be considered for such a lesson and also, honestly, to try something new. "Okay, that's fine. When is she scheduled to see you?"

Zita answered me quickly, "Next week will be good. On Thursday. I will call her and let her know you can make it then."

I arrived that day to find Lisa, and her mother, sitting in the parlor discussing the beautiful settings used in the Broadway production of *Cats*. I figured her mother would leave once we got started, but no … she stayed and watched us a little too closely for my comfort.

Lisa and I hit it off nicely. She was pretty, with blonde hair and blue eyes, and she had a relaxed manner along with a good sense of humor. *What was not to like?* We read well together, and I considered that she had a good degree of talent which, like me, was being fine-honed via Zita's professional guidance. *Unlike me,* however, with my career aspirations, it did not seem likely to me that Lisa wanted to pursue a career in showbiz. We had several conversations between our scenes, and I got the impression that she was more interested in settling down. Nevertheless, we laughed frequently at odd things, mostly our takes on the different characters, each other's increasingly wild gestures, and Zita's persistent attention to detail, and I found that I was enjoying her company.

This rapport between us had gotten her mother's attention, which, in turn, *led to me being put in my place.* She pulled me aside to the corner of the parlor room after one of the scenes Lisa and I had performed. "Tom, you seem like a nice enough man, however, please do not ever consider dating my daughter. It simply will not do." As she continued the conversation, I got the impression that Lisa's mother was more interested in seeing her daughter married off to a man of means. In any event, she made no bones about letting me know how ungodly it would be for me to even think, for just a second, about making a pass at her daughter. It also became clear that she was a very religious woman, almost to the extreme, and when I looked over my shoulder at Lisa and Zita talking on the couch, I knew right away that Lisa was embarrassed by her mother's conversation with me.

So now, I had not just one, but two adult women with major connections to God surrounding me, and somehow, I was the odd man out, even though I was raised Catholic and knew all about prayer and what could become of a non-believer. For some strange reason, I found myself telling Lisa's mother this, but it did not matter to her. The bottom line was that I was not adequate suitor material, and frankly, this did not bother me in the least. Zita never inquired thereafter, and I always wondered what Lisa's mother might have said to her about me - and if Zita herself had somehow prompted all of this by entertaining the idea of me being "boyfriend material" for Lisa in the first place. I did manage to maintain a brief *friendship* with Lisa and that was all, but I was glad for it just the same.

Several weeks thereafter, Zita and I sat in the parlor room for a bit of rest during one of our regular sessions. I could feel the cold drafts coming into the room from the outside gusts of fresh Canadian air and was happy when Zita offered a cup of hot tea. Returning from the kitchen with a cup for me and one for herself, she suddenly asked how I enjoyed my training with Lisa. This caught me off-guard, but I said that I thought it went very well and considered bringing up Lisa's mother's admonishment to me. Zita nodded, but I caught a fleeting glimpse of a far-away smile crossing her features, which intrigued me. As much as I was curious about what she was thinking, I decided to give it no further pursuit. Whenever I had inquired about any of her own suitors in the past, Zita had changed the subject at once, *and so why should I bring up anything further about my own personal issues?*

And then Zita surprised me once again when she

suddenly offered, "You know, Tom, I can remember

many of my own first outings with men. My mother, just

like Lisa's, was always present."

Although lately we had pursued a few minor

conversations here and there about her career and life in

NYC, it was general things, like how beautiful the

displays in the store windows were, some of her favorite

restaurants, and how people had dressed. And even if she

was just fishing and trying to get me to discuss my

experiences with Lisa *and her mother*, I felt like Zita had

just given me an opening and so I jumped in.

"Zita, I had been wondering about your own

romantic interests. I'd love to hear about your very first

crush." I was prepared for Zita to either ignore my

question or refuse to talk about it, but instead, she finally

was in the mood to entertain my curiosity.

"Well, that's easy." She paused and I could see she was thinking about how best to present the storyline. Crossing her legs with her left foot over her right knee, she continued, "You know, Tom, they say that a young girl's matinee idol is a first crush and never forgotten, and I think that is very true. Even though I was only eighteen at the time, my first crush was Basil Sydney. He was young and as handsome as they come, and he was an established actor - in fact, he was in many of the movies my friends and I would go to see on Saturday afternoons." She closed her eyes, and I could tell she was bringing to mind some happy memories. "You see, Tom, he was also a director and producer who was casting the upcoming season for the Theater Guild, and *it was this very audition I was hurrying my way to….*" She smiled and began kicking the air with her left foot. "Well, as luck would have it, I wound up on the same elevator as

207

Basil. *Can you imagine?* There I was looking up and suddenly seeing my very favorite idol staring right back at me!"

I smiled and shook my head in wonder, trying to think how I would feel should I ever be in such close proximity to Olivia Newton-John or Travolta. I could only imagine how this must have felt for Zita, who was trying to land a spot in the very theater that her idol was casting, directing, and producing. *"That is outrageous, Zita!* I can only imagine how this must have felt for you," I said. Although she had mentioned Basil to me while discussing how she had made it as an actress months before, this seemed much more personal this time around, and I had a feeling she was about to open up about more of the events during this time in her life. I might have been overstepping my boundaries, but I decided to risk taking things a step further. "Were you ever a couple? I bet y'all could have taken Manhattan by storm!"

"No, no… not at all. I got the part in the guild, and we got along famously, but we kept things strictly professional between us." There was brief silence and I wondered if that was all she was going to divulge even though it had not been much at all. Then it happened, Zita took it a step further without my prompting her. "You know, Tom, he wasn't the only man in my life at the time." She brought a bit of a mischievous glint to her eyes and her lips quivered a bit, and I knew it was about to get good.

She carefully sipped her tea and then placed the cup back down onto its saucer on the end table. I chanced a quick sip from my own cup and when she started, I found my fingers clasping the cup quite tightly. "You see, Tom, it was 1928, and I was playing a character in a play called "Machinal" which the Theater Guild was putting on at the time. I was cast as the love interest for one of the main characters - he was played by an up-and-coming actor by the name of Clark Gable, perhaps you have heard of him?"

I smiled and laughed at the same time. "Clark Gable, of course I've heard of him, Zita!" I was thinking, *not a bad way to get things going for your career.* She had mentioned having worked with him before, *but she had never informed me she had played his love interest.* And she just kept on going, like a trickle turning to a flood from a crack in a dam. It seemed that many good looking and talented men who were just starting out in the acting profession had found their way onto the stage with Zita.

"Soon after, I met John Houseman during another production. He was Romanian-born, believe it or not."

"I didn't know that."

"Yes, he was born Jacques Haussmann; spelled H-a-u-s-s-m-a-n-n, and he was known mostly as a British-American actor, and a great producer of theater and film. But as sure as I was an Austrian-American actress, he was Romanian-American by way of England." I smiled at her fun facts, which seemed to hold some added meaning and importance to Zita, and then I figured it would have to most of the biggest stars during the heydays of Hollywood, when so many actors of various ethnicities were making it big all at once. "Well, as I had already told you," Zita continued, "that was when Hollywood called for me via the attention of yet another handsome figure named Irving Thalberg, from MGM." I nodded as I recalled Zita's testimony months ago about the contract she had signed. "Mother and I had headed out west for six months to fulfill the contract that was offered, *but I was not thrilled in the least with the scripts* and returned back to New York. That was when I started to date John Houseman in earnest."

Just then Brandy came over, resting his chin on my lap, and I began rubbing his head. I realized my fascination with the men Zita worked with, along with those she had become romantically involved with, was unabashedly written across my face, and Zita obliged my desire to hear more. "There were so many men whom you've probably heard tell of, and others you may not have. I was very active in theater and had experiences with most of the biggest names. Basil Sydney, Clark Gable, Eddy Robinson, and D.W Griffith were always very professional in their working relationships with me, and believe me, I have come to appreciate that now in my later years."

"Yes, I can imagine that would be very important for a young actress just getting into the industry," I acknowledged.

"Yes! Well, Tom, let me assure you - I did not remain all about complete and absolute innocence myself for very long. At some point, I thought I would enjoy married life. When mother and I returned to New York, John and I dated for several months. *I then married Mr. Houseman.*" I wanted to hear all about what their marriage was like - two stars living in the big city, circa mid-1930's, this was pure gold to me and the stuff of legend. But that was all I was going to get, as her next words were, "Well, needless to say, we soon divorced."

I wanted to ask what had gone wrong in their relationship, but Zita was not about to get into any of that and never gave me the opportunity. She smiled and shook her head emphatically. "I then married producer

213

John McCormick and divorced him. Then, lastly, I married Bernard Shedd and … as you might guess, *that's right*, I divorced him."

I did not know how to respond or react to this in any appropriate manner. *What do you say to something like that? Zita, you must have found all the wrong ones? Zita, what did you do to drive them all away?* I found myself calling upon memories of all of my previous stage roles in hopes of finding a clue to deliver a suitable response at that moment. But none came to the surface in time, and by then, it did not matter, Zita was already moving on.

"You might find this interesting, Tom. When I married Bernard, the service and reception were held *right here at this house!* I can still picture all of it as if it was only yesterday. Everything was so beautiful at that time."

I took a moment to look around trying to picture all of the grand festivities of that day. It was a bit difficult seeing how much disrepair surrounded us, but finally, I saw elegant gowns and tuxedos adorning the most memorable actors from the first half of the nineteenth century. There would have been long tables of the best food all professionally displayed on silver trays, and the priciest champagne bottles would be sprouting from a multitude of ice buckets on their stands in every room. A state-of-the-art stereo system would have been belting out Frank Sinatra's *"Night and Day,"* and laughter would be coming from every area of the house and yard, as if nothing in the entire world could ever go wrong again.

Shaking me out of my reverie, I heard Zita saying, "Well, Tom, that is enough reminiscing for the time, don't you think?"

And I must admit, by now, yes, I had heard

enough. I was tired and needed to get home for dinner.

We ended our lesson that day with Zita providing

me with some overall feedback, and she seemed very

pleased with the progress I was making. Her

acknowledgement of my professional growth affirmed

the satisfaction I felt with the work we had been doing,

along with the time I was devoting to all of these lessons.

* * *

It had been a long, cold, but fulfilling winter

between work, my lessons, and keeping my social

calendar lit up. The following spring, the lessons

continued on, and I felt like I was learning something

new each time, even if it was just a tidbit of information

to carry me through in my understanding of how to expand my acting skills.

At the same time, I was advancing my skills as an actor, I was learning that I could never be sure what would happen next with Zita. As with the scene in the grocery store and with the cookies in my car, Zita was always just a stone's throw away from catching me by surprise, and then leaving me to wonder what to make of each new twist.

With another warm spring flourishing across the Lower Hudson Valley, we were just finishing a lesson and Zita had given me her targeted feedback when she wandered into the kitchen. I followed behind her and Zita walked over to the kitchen sink which looked out into the backyard. She stood there with her hands on either side of the ceramic basin and scanned the landscape beyond the window before turning back around to face me.

"You know, Tom, the lawn really needs to be mowed. It's quite overgrown now and definitely in need of some care."

I looked over her shoulder and out the window.

"Well, yes, Zita. I suppose it does. When was the last time you had someone over here to take care of it?"

"Oh, it's been a while." Zita turned back to face me, then tilted her chin and raised an eyebrow before moving to the kitchen table and taking a seat.

"I wouldn't wait too much longer before calling someone to take care of it, Zita. It will just make it more difficult for them to cut when they finally do so. Do you have the number of someone to call?" I was just trying to be supportive and helpful. I had no idea that I had just taken the bait and had walked myself right into her waiting trap.

"Actually, *I do,*" Zita chuckled slightly. "I was thinking this was something you would take care of for me in exchange for another free lesson."

I am sure my face must have registered at least a little of the surprise I was feeling, but I tried to recover quickly. "Oh, well, that is an idea, Zita." It took me no time at all to decide that I was not the least bit interested in mowing her lawn, but at the same time, I did not want to make a move that would upset the balance of our relationship. "I am not sure I can handle that, Zita, but I'll go outside and take a look around for you," and with that, I opened the kitchen door and waltzed out into the yard. I needed some time to think about how best to respond, but for now, I put on a contemplative face - one consistent with analyzing the yard for best possible cutting procedures.

I had not gone more than a few feet when the reality of the situation became even more painful for me. Zita's lawn was in dire need of help, but it would take a team of workers to begin taming all of the wilderness I was seeing upon closer inspection. There were branches and twigs covering the grounds which had fallen from the ancient trees and the overgrown shrubs strewn throughout the yard. I picked up a few and tossed them into a makeshift pile beneath a pine tree. The grass was tall, thick, and unruly, with even larger weeds sprouting up everywhere, and no doubt it would take a lot of equipment and the know-how of a professional landscaper to return it to a reasonably manicured condition.

I wasn't about to spend the amount of time it would take laboring in her yard; and the more I looked it over, I found myself becoming increasingly unsettled and disappointed. *This was not at all the direction I expected our arrangement to take.* I felt confused about Zita's request, maybe even slightly angered by it, and worse than that was the fact that I did not know how best to navigate her request, and so I took my time returning to the kitchen.

I walked over to the garage and opened the door to take a look inside. Where most garages are packed-full of stored items, Zita's garage had the bare minimum: one lone, gas-powered lawn mower. I stood looking across the empty space and couldn't help but let my imagination wander a bit. During one of our outings over the winter, Zita had told me about her prized 1957 Cadillac Fleetwood which had been stored in this garage for years. Before I came along, there was a hired driver who would take her on errands and who looked after the maintenance of the luxury automobile. In my mind, I saw him there in the garage beside the car, dressed in black pants and a crisp white shirt, leaning over as he methodically rubbed wax into the hood. Of course, the chrome trim on the car would have been glistening brightly as Zita walked up to him dressed in her finest peach-colored blouse and matching pants as she said, *"We must be off to the bank, Willard."*

Willard would have stopped polishing the hood immediately as he ran around the front of the car and opened the passenger-side door for Zita. *"Very well, Ma'am! We are ready!"*

Then I thought how sad it must have been for Zita when she finally decided to let the driver go, claiming she could no longer afford to keep him on considering the sporadic trips they made. Perhaps it was just a good business decision on her part, but knowing about Zita's propensity for drama, I could not help but wonder if that was the sole reason for the change. Of course, without a driver, Zita was left to her own devices and was soon driving herself to the post office or grocery store. Standing there looking into the ill-lit garage, I imagined tiny five-foot, four-inch Zita climbing into that monster vehicle, one big enough to hold eight people, and perching herself confidently behind the steering wheel. I had to laugh to myself as the image came clearly into view. In my mind, I could just see her taking great delight in smiling and waving at people as she drove that car into town, causing a spectacle wherever she went.

Even those days eventually had to come to an end. To her credit, not long before I made my arrival, Zita had acknowledged that it was time for her to get off the road as a driver, and so she had sold the car. Standing there in the empty garage, I thought about Zita and how she lived her life standing firm in her decisions, doing those things that she chose to do and letting go of the rest. I respected that about her; however, I then realized that very convicted trait of hers was contributing to why I was still grappling with how to tell her I would not be the answer to her landscaping needs.

I took a little more time wandering around the property and next headed toward the guesthouse to have a peek inside. I closed my hands around my face and stuck my head against the window - a lone shaft of sunlight was streaming in through the window in the far wall. From the looks of it, I could tell that it had been a long time since any guest had stayed there. The walls were in need of fresh paint and there were water stains on the ceiling from past leaks. The floor was littered with a cast-off newspaper, and a thick layer of dust had settled on top of the furniture. To my utter dismay, cobwebs filled gaps between the furniture and the walls, and also stood strong in the corners of the room between the walls and ceiling. *Clearly there was work to be done everywhere I turned; how was Zita possibly going to manage keeping this homestead from falling into further disrepair?*

I just shook my head and headed back toward the main house. When I looked up, I saw that Zita was staring at me from her perch at the kitchen window. As I came across the backyard towards her, I picked up some more small branches and twigs that surrounded me and contributed to my first pile beneath the pine tree. *I was not even beginning to put a dent into what needed to be done, and this job would be way too big for any single person. Frankly, I just did not want to get involved with any of it!*

I finally decided my best approach was to be direct. "Zita," I began to voice my concerns as soon as I came through the door to the kitchen. "I am not going to be able to mow your lawn for you."

"Oh. Well, *why not?*" Zita's eyes opened wide, and she seemed taken back by my statement.

"First of all, Zita, with all due respect," I began, "I don't mind driving you on your errands and helping you with little things around the house as needed, but this job is just too much for one person. And in all honesty, I don't have any interest in doing this kind of work. If I had, I could be making good money as a landscaper."

Zita sat down once again at the kitchen table and as she did so, she emitted a loud "Hmph" which reverberated her displeasure quite distinctly.

I felt sure that anything else I could add at the moment would only trigger further dissension between us. "I need to take off, Zita. I'll see you again Thursday." And with those words, I made a hasty retreat back to my car. I thought about her request and my negative reaction to it all the way home. The last thing I wanted to do was to irritate Zita and possibly upset what we had going on with our bartering agreement for my extra lessons, but I *was not* second-guessing my decision to draw the line against manual labor, and I thought my response to her set an appropriate boundary.

Thursday came and I felt sure that whatever awkwardness had transpired between us could be cleared up, and I felt eager to return to my acting lessons. Our lesson that day started off in its usual manner: I once again drove Zita to the bank and the post office. She didn't mention anything about my refusal to mow the lawn, and I didn't bring it up either. Things seemed okay and I was grateful for that. After completing her errands, we returned to Zita's house.

I helped Zita with the car door and walked beside her up the front sidewalk of the house. She made her way up the three steps of the front porch and stopped when she reached the porch itself, resting her hands on the railing. I thought she might be resting for a spell and so I came up the steps and then stood beside her. "Look at this porch," she said.

I moved my eyes back and forth, taking in the peeling paint and dingy look of the columns and railings. *My heart skipped a beat because I suddenly had a bad feeling about what she might say next.*

And then it came! "When you paint this porch for me, there will be another lesson in it for you," declared Zita. She made this statement without the least hint of it being a question, but rather a done deal that was non-negotiable.

With all of the determination I could muster, I said, "Now, Zita, this is a large porch and a really big job. I don't like to, or know much about, painting at all."

"Well, you will learn how to do it and learn how to like painting just as well as you will mowing; *they're just not that difficult to accomplish,*" Zita responded without a bit of hesitation in her voice.

It seemed clear that her mind was made up and that there was to be no further discussion. This turn of events surprised and confounded me so much that I had no idea what to say next. I was all too eager to let the conversation drop, and so I did. Thankfully we headed into the house without another word said about it.

Our lesson that day focused on *Hamlet*, and even though I typically enjoyed these readings, I found my mind drifting much too often and could not focus on my characters. I just could not allow myself to fall into any of the roles as readily as I had been, nor could I concentrate on the words I was speaking. After just ten minutes of this, I was thinking that this lesson could not come to an end soon enough. Finally, it did, and at that point, I chose not to engage in any small talk with Zita for fear that it might give her the opportunity to bring up her household maintenance needs once again. And so, at the end of the lesson, I quickly got to my feet and hurried to the front door. Before exiting, I turned and said, "See you next time, Zita," and I did not wait for her response.

All the way home, our conversation on the porch repeatedly ran through my mind. Zita had made her position clear, and this was bothering me to no end. *What in the hell is going on? Why would she expect me to take on such big jobs?* Even if I wanted to do them, which I didn't, I would not be able to do them without help. *Surely, she understands that. Just what direction is she expecting our relationship to take?*

I was so confused and unsettled about Zita's proposals that I decided to get another opinion. I knew my mom would give me some honest feedback, and so I told her what had transpired during my last two lessons with Zita. We sat at the kitchen table, each of us cradling a cup of mom's fresh, hot coffee.

"Something kind of strange happened at Zita's, and I am not sure what to make of it."

"Well, tell me about it." My mom sat across from me and in her usual motherly manner, she began carefully slicing the warm pecan pie she had recently removed from the oven.

"On Tuesday afternoon, after our lesson, she suggested that I mow her huge yard in exchange for another extra lesson. Zita's lawn is massive! With all of the weeds growing, the branches scattered everywhere, and everything else ... *it hasn't been groomed in such a long time,* so it would be very time-consuming and difficult, even for a team of landscapers."

My mom nodded her head in agreement. She slipped me a plate loaded with a slice of pie and a fork. "What did you tell her?"

"I was honest. I told her the job was just too big for one person and anyway, that I was not happy doing that kind of work at all." I took a bite of my pie and realized how comforting my mom's cooking has always been - the pie was delicious, as usual, and she smiled at me knowing how much I was enjoying it. Then I continued my story. "I thought I had set an appropriate boundary and that she accepted my answer, but then today, after coming from her errands at the post office and bank, *she asked me to paint her porch.* Again, it would be a very large job - the old paint needs to be scraped off, I would need ladders and tarps, and I am just not into doing that kind of work."

My mom shook her head as she tried a bite of her pie.

"I told her I could not do it," I continued. "Then she even went so far as to say that I will learn to enjoy painting as much as mowing the grass and that neither was that difficult!" By now, my blood pressure was rising once again just reliving the tension Zita had introduced into our relationship.

My mom put her fork down and looked at me directly. "Tom, it seems like she needs a houseboy or a handyman *and is expecting you* to fill that role for her."

I was taken back by my mom's blunt perspective and immediately felt defensive, probably because I wanted to defend Zita for some reason, although at this point, I was still unaware of why that might be. "No, I don't think that's it. She just needs help around the property and maybe I'm an easy target because she knows how eager I am for more lessons."

"I don't know, Tom," my mom replied. We ate more of our pie slices silently for a few moments. "Just give it some thought, will you? Remember why you are there in the first place."

"Okay, I will," I answered and then I thanked my mom for listening. I spent a lot of time over the next few hours considering my relationship with Zita. I found myself moving through anger at her, and then feeling like she was trying to take advantage of me for my kindness. *Even if I somehow found a way to help her mow and paint, would those projects be the end of her requests? Would I be unclogging toilets next? Scrubbing her oven? Doing her laundry? Where would it all end?*

That's when I realized it would never end. *She would always push and push, always telling me I would "learn to like" whatever task she next set before me....*

Over the weekend, I alternated between obsessing about the situation with Zita and trying my best to distract myself from thinking about her altogether. One of the things I wanted most from Zita was to hear about her days in Hollywood, which I found to be so interesting and inspiring. But she only gave me tiny bits of information on her own terms, mostly about her theatrical work in New York, and the truth was, Zita didn't like reminiscing much about making the movies which had earned her the larger portion of her fame. I only saw the parts of her past that could be romanticized and seen through rose-colored lenses - the fragments of an acting career which made her look fabulous, without much of the reality behind any of it. Even at this age and stage of her life, *what was she hiding so dearly, and why was she still so insistent on hiding from it?* That's when it hit me: *I have gotten from Zita all that I can hope to get. It might be time for me to move on.*

Over that weekend, something did happen which helped me make my final decision about what to do regarding Zita. I was introduced to the industry casting paper *"Backstage."* Included in that paper was a list of open calls for film and television parts, as well as contact information for photographers and acting classes. I chose a photographer and had my first professional headshots done. Next, I started searching for an acting class that would work for my schedule. The week ahead held great promise and I felt I was finally gaining momentum in developing my future in the business. I also thought of the conversation I would have with Zita, and by now had made the decision to no longer continue my lessons with her. *I needed to move on, and I planned to tell her that straight out.* Taking these steps that weekend had independently confirmed for me that I was ready to move forward, beyond Zita; *now I just needed to tell her my plans.*

On Tuesday afternoon, I returned to Zita's house. She welcomed me in and we had a seat in the living room. "Zita, I need to talk to you about something."

"That's fine, Tom. Can it wait, though, until after our lesson today?"

I looked at Zita and spoke with conviction. "Actually, I am not staying for a lesson, Zita. In fact, I won't be able to take any more lessons with you."

Zita's chin tilted upward, and she questioned me with a slight glare in her eyes, "What do you mean? *Why not?*"

"I just won't be able to do it anymore. This is the last time I will be able to come by." I offered no explanation and kept my tone devoid of emotion. I was still angry at her for assuming I would become the caretaker for her residence, which, *I would realize later on,* made me feel like she was not taking my acting career as seriously as I had presumed that she had been for the past year. At that moment, all I knew was that I was being very abrupt, and that I felt betrayed by her somehow. I didn't know why and could not put a finger on it - I was only twenty-two at the time and not in the habit of thinking things all the way through.

She was crestfallen in any regards. *"I thought you said I was like a grandmother to you;* what can you possibly mean that this is the last time you will be able to come by?"

Once again, I answered robotically and without much compassion. "I just won't be able to continue doing this."

Now, she became angered. "What!? *I should slap your face!* Well, if that is how you feel, you should leave now."

Without another word I stood from my chair, walked briskly to the door, closed it gently behind me, and then trod down the steps of the aging house toward my car. As I started the engine, I chuckled about Zita saying she should slap my face, because in typical Zita fashion, she had proclaimed this with great theatrical delivery. Behind the humor, though, I was feeling a sense of relief, but it came coupled together with a growing twinge of guilt. Since I was just twenty-two at the time, my main focus was that *I had accomplished exactly what I had set out to do.*

No more worry over how to turn down the next big chore. Zita could dangle anything in front of me, *and now I was free from it and free from my obligation to her.* With that concern taken care of, I realized almost immediately that I had not considered how I might have just made Zita feel.

But again, I was young, a little self-centered, and in my mind, done with Zita as my mentor. Her terms of our relationship had changed but mine hadn't. I tried putting all of it out of my mind for now because it was time to get ready to move onto the next summer adventure....

***

Chapter Eight

Steve

***

In November of that year, I moved into my first apartment in Manhattan, a big step for me. The fast pace and excitement of city life made for a rigorous challenge compared to the relatively slower pace of the suburbs, but I found it exhilarating. I now felt I was living in an environment conducive to my career, surrounded by other actors hoping to get their big breaks while being in close vicinity to theaters, agents, and everyone else involved in the industry, for that matter.

For the next two years, I kept myself busy with a variety of theater projects in addition to being introduced to work as a background artist in film while also securing a few bit parts on television. I met a few other thespians who, like me, were all struggling to carve their paths along the way to becoming successful actors. Some of these, I still keep in touch with now and again through social media. But even though I was living in NYC, I stayed in touch with everyone at home and made it a point to visit from time to time.

Funny how old attachments never really go away no matter how busy we may become and how many new attachments we've forged. Amidst the fond recollections of my past training, mixed with thoughts of her zealous outbursts, her candor and scornful demanding, and now my own guilt due to not wanting to feel as if I had abandoned her altogether, Zita had never remained very far away from me. That is what brought me back to her house. The guilt from my quick "exit stage left" had been lingering for quite some time. *Was she lonely with nobody to look after her? Did she have anyone helping her with weekly chores? When I left, did I leave her all by herself and helpless?*

I had arranged it with Zita that I would pay her a visit on one of my trips back home - I had to check in to make sure that she was okay. When I finally made the commitment to go and visit her, something had suddenly overtaken me, and I felt just like the prince who needed to run in to save the "damsel in distress" living trapped in her ivory tower.

As I drove along Route 9w northwards to West Nyack, I thought about all of our most personal conversations about the men from her past. She had a habit of keeping the past, *men included*, tucked safely away, rarely sharing names and secrets, and I considered myself lucky to have heard the bits of her history that she had shared. Recalling these moments as I pulled into Zita's driveway, I may have been gone for almost two years, but I still felt melancholy about the end of my time with her. I noticed immediately that the yard was in no better repair than it had ever been during the time of my lessons - still overgrown with weeds sprouting in abundance, last autumn's leaves in large clusters, and those dead branches everywhere.

In any case, here I was again, back in her driveway, feeling as if no time had passed at all. As I made my way to the front door, Zita once again called out to me from an upstairs window, saying she would be right down. I came up the porch steps and saw that no work had been done anywhere on the porch since I had left, and so I stood there, waiting patiently, just like I did on the day of my very first visit.

Finally, Zita opened the door. I smiled and said hello, and waited for a moment, but she didn't ask me in. Even though she offered a slight brightening of her expression, immediately I felt that she was being standoffish. In the next moment, I found myself reflecting on our last conversation, and so her reaction was somewhat understandable to me. Looking back, I wasn't sure why I had been so abrupt with terminating our mentorship without offering Zita anything more in the way of information in terms of my feelings at the time.

"It's so good to see you, Zita," I said. "How are you doing?"

"Just fine." Zita answered without hesitation. She examined me up and down and her expression became like one of those stoic Greek statues depicting a woman scorned. "I have a nice man, Steve, living in the guesthouse," she said, and the line seemed as if it had been rehearsed (actually, I don't remember if she said his name, but from here on, I will call him Steve). "He is a big help getting things done around the yard." I looked at her and had to stifle a grin but chose not to argue with her. "He needed a place to live because he was living out of his van. Someone I know suggested we could help one another."

Really, I did not know what to say. However, these were the words which came tumbling out: "Well, that sounds like it's a good situation for you, Zita. I'm glad you are doing so well." Even as I said that I doubted the guest house had been worked on since nothing else had been. Last I had seen, it was still in need of repair and not fit for anybody to live in. *I soon realized that I*

246

was obsessed. I had to find out if it had been given any care. Since I could tell that no work had been done on the inside or outside of the house, it made me wonder, was this guy Steve living out of his van? It did strike me as an odd situation.

That's when I realized our conversation lacked any sense of warmth, and it was becoming very awkward almost instantly. She never asked me how I was doing, or what I was doing, and after a bit of silence, I discussed a few of my most recent projects very briefly. She nodded and that was it.

"Well, I am so glad you are doing well, Zita," I repeated, uncertain where else to go with the discussion. Again, she nodded and then the silence returned between us. It was the type of silence that is louder than screaming, and I found that it deafened me. I nodded and smiled, and then our conversation ended pretty quickly thereafter.

"Oh well, I wish you the best," she exclaimed in a voice that was unusually monotone for Zita, after only what amounted to a few minutes of extremely superficial conversation.

"You as well, Zita. I will come by and say hello another time when I am home if that's okay?"

"That's fine," Zita said, and with that she headed back inside and closed the door to her house.

I headed back down the steps, feeling in the moment as disappointed in my actions from two years ago as Zita obviously still was. Our relationship, I realized, would never be as friendly as it once had been, and this caused me great discontent. I scanned the property and took a long loop to get back to my car, and that is when I noticed the older model van parked alongside the guesthouse. Sure enough, the building was as dilapidated as ever and still in need of much repair. It certainly didn't look fit for anybody to be living in it. *If he were still living in his van, what use would Steve be getting out of this arrangement?* I suddenly wished I had pushed a little bit to get more information about Steve, but at the same time, I was sure she would have become bored with my inquiry and perhaps even have put a quicker end to my visit. I knew it wasn't really any of my business, although it seemed like an odd situation to me. Bottom line, since Zita had seemed comfortable with it, *that was that.*

As I got in my car and sat quietly before starting the engine, I gazed up at her windows and had the feeling that I would soon also become one of the men in Zita's past. She didn't like to talk about them because they were in the past and that is where she kept them, tucked away, the names and secrets of lives gone by. The excruciating and specific terms and conditions which by and large became the price for endearing oneself to Zita: *that was for each man alone to know, to weigh, and then to decide if it was worth the cost.*

As I drove off to enjoy the rest of the remaining summer days, I had the thought that it always seemed as if it had been the summertime when I was most involved in Zita's life. I could have titled this novella, *My Summers with Zita*, but they were simply just not those kinds of summers.

I drove south on Route 9w that afternoon with quite a few mixed emotions. I did not regret having ended my lessons with Zita under the circumstances of two years ago, but I did regret the cavalier way I treated her on that last afternoon. She deserved more than that, and it seemed like the kind of mistake that would not be easy to rectify. On top of that, I was bothered by the situation with Steve, even though I knew very few details. But due to the current status of our relationship, I felt I was not in the position to probe Zita about whether or not the choices she was making were in her best interest. My questions would, unfortunately, have to remain unanswered, at least for the time being.

Having moved into the city, I was taking advantage of many things. Every day I found myself rubbing elbows with other actors, people involved in production crews, as well as filmmakers. This close proximity to other professionals made it easy for me to find work on projects with a decent budget and enjoy getting paid on a union salary scale. The first movie that I worked background on was "Cadillac Man" with Robin Williams in 1989. I was also cast in a successful Off-Broadway comedy called *Grandma Sylvia's Funeral,* and

251

this gave me a sense of confidence I hadn't felt before. I was truly relishing in all of the opportunities coming my way.

At the same time, I landed a job as a bartender at a popular Upper East Side restaurant on East 58th Street called *The Townhouse*. The restaurant was within walking distance from my apartment, and I loved the convenience of having a job so close to my living quarters at 430 East 65th Street. I was able to keep myself busy with both furthering my career and doing work which allowed me to engage with many interesting people. I needed both incomes, since living in NYC is an extremely expensive endeavor.

Looking back at this time in my life, I am not sure why I thought my status was such that I needed to have my phone number unlisted, but it was something that I felt compelled to do. The phone company told me there would be a yearly charge for un-listing my number, however, and I wasn't about to pay for that service. So, I figured out a loophole and just shortened my last name to Ford which rendered me technically "unlisted" because the actual phone book now listed a Tom Ford at E65th and not me, Tom Stratford. *Genius move, or so I thought.*

One day I arrived home to see the little red light on my answering machine blinking away, and I quickly pressed the button for the message. In the background, I heard what I would describe as some cosmic Zen-type music and the message was delivered by a woman with a similarly mystical quality.

"Tom Ford, we are destined to meet. The stars have sent me to you through our mutual respect for design; we should collaborate on our talents because the stars and the cosmic forces suggest so." For three minutes, I listened to this transcendent voice explaining there was a connection that had been *written in the stars* between herself and Tom Ford. I chuckled a bit at the odd message but didn't spend too much time thinking about it until I listened to the second of the messages that my machine had preserved that afternoon. I immediately recognized the voice as belonging to the same woman, and this message was similar to the other: she wanted Tom Ford to know that each of their futures relied solely on the two of them meeting, *and this had been preordained by the universe itself.*

The following day, I ran into a friend of mine at the restaurant where I worked. When he asked me what was new in my life, I recounted the odd messages for Tom Ford. "Well, do you actually know who Tom Ford is?" he asked me, his eyebrows lifted in scrutiny.

"No, I have no idea who he is," I answered. "But I wonder if he is as strange as this woman seems to be."

My friend quickly filled me in. "Actually, the real Tom Ford is a well-known designer for the Gucci family, and he lives in this neighborhood."

"Oh, I guess that's impressive," I countered. "Now I am a little intrigued just thinking about the messages I might get by accident."

Sure enough, about a week later, the phone in my apartment rang. Each time it had done so since I had received those first two messages for the *other* Tom Ford, I picked up the receiver half-expecting that it would be the same mystical woman. This time, however, it was a very different female voice on the other end of the line. In a lovely Italian accent, this woman politely informed me that she was calling from Italy and was hoping to speak with Tom Ford. Now, I knew she wasn't actually looking for me, and so I explained the best I could about there being *two* Tom Fords on the Upper East Side.

She chuckled. "Do you know the other Tom?" she asked, her voice resonating with laughter.

"No, I only know that he designs for Gucci," I offered. And then, for what seemed like ten minutes or more, she told me how highly she thought of the other Tom Ford and all of his wonderful work. Eventually. I was able to interrupt her charming monologue long enough to make a suggestion. "It's been lovely talking to you, but I think perhaps you should call the other Tom Ford number before you rack up a huge charge for talking to the *wrong* Tom Ford."

She chuckled once again. "You are probably right," she said. And with that she wished me a good evening, and I wished her the same, before finally hearing the phone line click dead.

I shook my head and snickered to myself softly.

Boy, this real Tom Ford must live an interesting life.

Winters in New York City can get very cold, snowy, slushy, and messy. Salt spreaders throw salt all over the streets and sidewalks. What's not mushy brown slop soon turns to dirty white with the drying of shoe trails. Winds howl around buildings and snatch at you while you are walking, taking scarves, hats, and anything else not attached securely to your body whistling down the avenue. The constant cold and frequent snows are some of the things which can wear you down when living in the city.

However, I was only an hour away from my family, and when the winter finally started to ease a bit, I traveled home every other Sunday to enjoy some home cooking. I enjoyed the peace and quiet, and it was a nice change from what surrounded me in New York City each

257

and every day. My visits home allowed me to catch up with my family and to hear the most recent neighborhood gossip. Small towns are always ripe with tales about who was doing what with whom, who was thriving and doing well, whose family was in some sort of crisis, and who, if anyone, had taken a turn for the worse.

As spring came upon us, the bus ride to my parents' home was generally invigorating, especially as my favorite season was revving up. To me, springtime was full of promise for new beginnings, and the beautiful sights and familiar aromas of sprouting green landscapes and colorful flowers usually filled me with the anticipation of what might lie ahead in the days to come. *It was on a particularly warm and sunny afternoon, during one of these visits, that I once again felt the need to see Zita in order for us to catch up.*

I had called at the last minute to check if it was okay for me to drive over, and I experienced the same haunting feeling of separation-anxiety toward the end of my drive to Zita's house. *What would I find? How would she act towards me? What would her mental state be like this time around?* Coming down the driveway, the overgrown landscape was a little worse than before, and the worn-out conditions of the residence itself were a bit more abysmal than I had last seen them. *It still could be a stately home if only given some care,* and this thought only added to my painful nostalgia. Once again, Zita watched me from the second-floor window as I pulled my car up to the front of the driveway. She was no longer in the window as I got out of my car and climbed the steps of the front porch and waited for Zita to appear. She opened the door, and it took no time for me to register her lackluster enthusiasm upon seeing me.

"What did you want to see me for?" she asked, her voice a flat monotone of disinterest.

Her words seemed like a challenge to me and in response, I gave her a bright smile and answered as genuinely as I could. "I wanted to check in on you to see how you are doing and to make sure you are okay."

"Oh. Well, I'm just fine," Zita said. She made no move to invite me inside and showed no appreciation for my interest in her. "You know you don't have to do that," she continued, "I am doing just fine."

"I am glad to hear that, Zita," I said. I wondered what had happened with Brandy and Peanuts since they had not come to inspect who had come calling at the front door. Thinking about the three of them living alone here in this big house for some reason suddenly saddened me, and once again I felt those momentary pangs of guilt.

As I was about to ask about them, Zita surprised me by volunteering some new information. "Steve left. He just packed up and drove out without giving me any notice or explanation. He left no trail and no way to track him moving forward." For just a brief moment, she looked down at my feet, where the paint was peeling off the porch's wooden boards. Then she said, "And that's fine with me, really."

I felt my forehead crease a bit out of concern. "That's not fine! That must have been quite a shock, Zita, that he left *without saying anything to you.* Are you sure you feel okay about that?" I didn't expect her to change her report regarding how she felt about Steve's leaving, but I wanted her to at least know that I did care about her well-being and so it was not fine with me.

She looked like a little girl at that moment - just like a sad little girl who had just endured a terrible ordeal and could not make any sense of it. My heart fell to my feet as I stood there, because I feared what else she might tell me. "There is one more detail to this whole thing," she finally said.

I leaned in close, ready to extend a hand for support if she needed it. I looked into her eyes and tried to show a brave face, although my despair was not far from the surface.

Zita looked at me with tired eyes. "I had given him my *After the End* manuscript and screenplay to read, both of them." Her voice remained emotionless as she finished her admission. "He never gave them back and he didn't leave them behind." The look on her face matched her voice in its stoicism.

"But Zita," I countered, now furious. *"How could he?* Those were the only copies you had, right?" I felt enraged that her wonderful work had been taken and wiped away by some lowlife transient as she nodded.

"Did you call the police? What are you going to do about this?" By now, I am sure that my face had grown red with anger and frustration

"No. It's gone now, and there is nothing I can do about it." Zita was as passive as I had ever seen her - almost complacent. There was no hint of the dramatic display of emotion and language I had seen from her in times past. "It's gone and I am not worried. I can't do anything about it." She paused and looked into my eyes with firm conviction. *"Nothing will come of it, you see, Tom, because it was before its time."*

"But, Zita," I argued. "This is important. Your work is important. There has to be something you can do. Did he ever say anything to you about the script and what he thought of it? Did he mention having any connections within the film industry?" I was clearly more upset than she was, and I could not understand how she could just accept this without fighting to get her work back. *How could she have let this happen? Maybe I shouldn't have been so quick to part ways with her all those years back. Maybe I should have visited her more often.* I shook my head in disbelief, but mostly guilt was now flooding my thoughts.

Zita waved her hand in the air as if she was tossing birdseed to the ground. "Just forget about it. What's done is done, and this is the way it was supposed to be."

"No, Zita," I implored. "This is not the way it is supposed to be." In my mind, I was running through all the possible ways of tracking this thief down. "Where did Steve live when he was a child?"

"Tom," she said, her voice growing weary with frustration. "Once again, you're not listening to me. This is what the Gods had in store; do you understand? Nothing will happen with my book or screenplay while they are in the wrong hands. They are before their time, and my story won't work in those other hands. I am sure of that."

I didn't want to just let it go, but it was obvious that my questions came across to Zita like an over prodding parent to a bullied teenager, and I soon realized she had no use for my investigation. *Perry Mason would have handled this differently,* I thought, but I had already blown my chance to elicit her cooperation. The more I pushed and prodded, asked and insisted, I realized that Zita's acceptance of what had happened was not going to change and I was just pushing her away. She was tired of me, tired of my reaction to her having been victimized, and I knew it was time to say yet another goodbye.

"Well, anyway, I am sorry for what happened." I shook my head and had no other words for her. "You take care, okay?" I turned and began my walk back to my car. I had the immediate sense that this would be my last visit with Zita. I reached for my door handle and took one last look over my shoulder. Zita was already back inside her house. *There had been no final wave or dismissal.*

Pulling back down the driveway, I felt beaten, confused, and at a loss for what to do. I felt solely responsible for how things had played out. Her great work and her great love, *After the End,* was gone now. It had vanished into the hands of a common low-life transient, someone who could do whatever he pleased with its ideas, its characters, and its genius. Having spent so many hours with those wonderfully complicated and nuanced characters under the watchful eyes of their creator, my mentor Zita, it was with a heavy heart when I realized I had lost something and someone very special. Driving home, *I knew with certainty that this was the end, and I had just completed my last visit with Zita.*

***

I returned to my life in the city, and things kept getting busier in both my professional and personal lives. I faced my share of disappointments, failures, and sweet successes, as do most of us in life. I maintained my determination to succeed as an actor, and my skill set increased with each and every experience. Often, I would recall, and then use, something Zita had instilled in me, and I realized that all of those lessons were paying off the further I immersed myself into the profession of acting. I found that I had a grasp of the craft that was well beyond most other actors who were at a similar level of experience, and though some of that was due to my determination to be the best, I must contribute a fair share of it to Zita's insights and training. Time itself flew by, and in the blink of an eye, years had passed.

Once a week, I would speak to my mom on the phone to catch-up, and sure enough, she would always tempt me with whatever tantalizing meal she had planned for that coming Sunday to make sure that I would be there sitting at her table. Roast beef was one of my weak spots (and still is). One particular phone call, however, seemed different from the start. I sensed that something had changed.

"Have you read anything about Zita recently?" my mom asked.

"No, I haven't," I answered.

"There was an article in the local paper, Tom. She passed away on September 24th."

I was crestfallen. It was September 1993, and immediately, my mind filled with so many thoughts and memories of Zita. I had known her for ten years, and now that she was no longer among the living, I felt a great loss. It was as if an immediate and deep void had appeared in the structure of my life itself. *She was gone. It was final. Zita would now only ever be just my memory of Zita.*

It was only minutes after ending the call with my mom that I knew something with absolute clarity. For my life to continue as seamlessly as possible, Zita would have to be more than just a memory: *she would have to be a memory I felt compelled to honor.* At the time, I had no idea how I would keep her memory alive or how I would introduce her to those who didn't know her, but I was sure this would be something I would find a way to do.

She had given me so much, and now I wanted to repay her.

I had found out about her passing too late to make any of the services for her. A week later, I found this article in the New York Times:

Zita Johann Dead; Actress, 89, Played The Mummy's Love

Zita Johann, a stage and film actress who played Boris Karloff's love interest in "The Mummy," died on Friday at Nyack Hospital in Nyack, N.Y. She was 89 and lived in Orangeburg, N.Y.

The cause was pneumonia, said a friend, Rosemary Franck.

Miss Johann was born near Temesvar, Hungary, now Timisoara, Romania. She moved to New York City with her family when she was 7 and appeared in high school productions. After applying to the Theater Guild for work as an understudy, she immediately won roles in touring productions of "Peer Gynt," "The Devil's Disciple" and "He Who Gets Slapped."

She made her Broadway debut in 1924 in the Theater Guild's production of "Man and the Masses." Other leading roles followed, in "Machinal" (1928), "Tomorrow and Tomorrow" (1931) and other plays. To Hollywood and Back

In 1931 she played the wife of a steelworker who succumbs to drink in "The Struggle," the last film by D. W. Griffith. Most memorably, she played Helen Grosvenor in "The Mummy" (1932), whom the Mummy takes to be the vestal priestess for whom he conceived a forbidden passion 3,700 years earlier.

After appearing in "Tiger Shark" (1932), "Luxury Liner" (1933) and "Grand Canary" (1934), she returned to New York to act in the

271

theater. She appeared in "Panic"
(1935), "Flight Into China"
(1939), "The Burning Deck"
(1940) and "The Broken Journey"
(1942).

During World War II, she raised
money for war-related charities
and organized shows for
American soldiers on their way
overseas. In recent decades, she
worked with disturbed children
and gave private acting lessons.

Her three marriages, to John
Houseman, the director, John
McCormick, an agent, and
Bernard E. Shedd, an economist
and publisher, all ended in
divorce.

She had no children. [1]

---

[1] Grimes, <u>William</u>. *Zita Johann Dead; Actress, 89, Played The Mummy's Love.* New York Times, Sept. 30, 1993. Accessed November 23, 2022.
https://www.nytimes.com/1993/09/30/obituaries/zita-johann-dead-actress-89-played-the-mummy-s-love.html

At the time, I did not know how to reach out to find what became of her estate or where she might have been buried. The internet was just beginning to come to our attention and most of us had no working knowledge about how to use it, and throughout the following weeks, I was extremely busy with my two work obligations. However, not a day passed when a memory of her presence while we were en route to one of her destinations, or processing through one of our training routines, did not filter through my mind.

It was a year later when I felt like Zita had just about *hand-delivered* the solution to my question of how I could repay her for all that she had done for me, and perhaps also make up for my part in having ended our relationship so abruptly. And it came, oddly enough, by way of Steve.

At the time I had emboldened myself to start trying my own hand at writing. I began with a treatment for a sitcom that I developed, and it was taking form pretty nicely. At night, I usually wrote with the television on for inspiration but with the volume down low. But this one night, for some reason, I left the volume turned up and decided to tune in to a new one-hour drama that one of the major networks was introducing. About three minutes into it, I felt the hair on my arms stand up. *It was uncanny.* Without a doubt, I knew I was watching Zita's work! This new drama was actually Zita's beloved *After the End.*

I literally jumped out of my chair and yelled at the television, *"That's Zita's work!"* I watched closely as the drama unfolded. There was no question about it... there were the delphiniums which adorned the bar, Michael the chauffeur was one of the main characters, a

274

glowing and ominous fog was used as a setting characterization for the surrounding area, and the lounge of the hotel was the shelter for twelve lost and misbegotten strangers. Some of the dialogue and clothing descriptions had even *been taken directly from Zita's pages!* I knew instantly that there was only one way Zita's work could end up on the network's new fall lineup. *I'll be damned.* Steve left with her manuscript and then when he knew she passed, he changed the author's name to his, taking ownership like it was his work, and he sold it.

Immediately, I began to research whatever information I could find about the show, but the information was limited. With no robust internet available, this was like finding a needle in a haystack. I had to wait for the next episode to air so that I could watch specifically for the credits. I wrote down as much as I could. And then, something unexpected happened. *The network canceled the show after only three episodes.*

I was in my living room when I read it in TV Guide the week after the third episode aired. Once again, the hair on my arms stood on end. It was just like Zita had told me on our last visit: *it wasn't going to work in the wrong hands. It was before its time!*

Despite the fact that the drama had been canceled, I was still bothered by what Steve had done and the fact that Zita's amazing work was not being seen and appreciated. *What can I do to right this wrong? How can I make sure Zita's work is honored and treasured?* It didn't surprise me that Zita would not remain just a memory. I kind of expected to hear from her. The surprise was how she came back to life, together with the message she was putting out to me and me only.

I opened a black and white speckled notebook and started writing everything I could remember about Zita, as well as everything I knew about the storyline for *After the End.* Many pages later, I put the notebook away in my desk drawer, feeling some sense of relief. It wasn't that I thought I had made everything right, but it was a start. So long as I felt I was keeping something of Zita moving forward, it was as if I had her permission to allow *myself to move forward.*

Once again, I focused on my own career as an actor, and I returned to fine-tune my original treatment for a television sitcom.

***

Epilogue

***

Almost 25 years had passed since I had spoken to anyone about my time with Zita and all that I had written about her in that little speckled black and white notebook. My career at the time, in 2017, had been going well. I was working doing a combination of background, feature, and bit parts. I had moved to Nyack in May of 2011, after subleasing my NYC apartment, and had even gone to LA for a few months in order to check out casting companies to see if it would be a good idea to start fresh on the West Coast. However, similar as with

Zita, it wasn't a good fit for me, and to answer one of

Zita's earlier questions, *No, you're right, Zita, I was not*

prepared for a big move like that.

As my work as an actor were all part-time and

temporary jobs, I still worked as a bartender, once again,

in a restaurant that was just a few blocks from my

apartment. It was a fun place to work, and the restaurant

was popular enough that I was often making new friends

and had plenty of regular customers.

One particular couple, Ron and Amy, became

quick friends of mine, and we would often talk about my

latest projects and what was next on my horizon. One

night I shared my Zita story with them, and they showed

immediate interest. Ron had worked as a writer and

comic book developer for years, and he had even helped

in writing the movie versions of several comic book

heroes. He suggested that I take all of the notes I had

about Zita, go through them, put them in order, and send them to him. He said he would then work on them to get them in the professional form that was needed in order to put my work in front of a publisher. Ron was busy with traveling to comic conventions since he was still a popular comic developer, and he also held seminars for upcoming writers. That was fine with me; he would get to my notes when he could. I was just excited that someone who was a professional in the publication field had taken an interest in my work.

In late November of that year, I started going over everything I had written, began rewriting it, and then sent my updates to Ron. He was busy traveling, but still made time for my updates and assured me that I had something good, especially my desire to find *After the End.*

As I was working on organizing my notes about Zita to send to Ron, I also tied up one other loose end from years back. This came in the form of a letter to the "other" Tom Ford.

Greetings Tom Ford-

My name is Tom Stratford and I live in Nyack NY. I am an actor currently working in and around New York. I am writing to you today in regards to my time living in the city during the 1990s at 430 E 65th, when I also worked part time at a popular restaurant on E 58th St. called The Townhouse.

During that time, I was cast in an off-Broadway show, and it was then I decided for some reason that my phone number needed to be unlisted. I was told by the phone company I would be charged yearly to be unlisted (which I thought was crazy), so to avoid the charge I shortened my last name to

Ford; therefore being "unlisted" in a sense. Now I was listed as Tom Ford E65th St.

At that time, I had no idea of who you were. It wasn't until the new phone book came out that I realized there were now two Tom Fords on the upper east side: you on 68th, and me on 65th. I didn't think much about it and left it at that until....

One day I returned home from work to find two messages on my answering machine. The first was from a woman and there was some cosmic Zen type of music playing in the background as she spoke. She said something like this - Tom Ford, we are destined to meet. The stars have sent me to you through our mutual respect for design, and we should collaborate on our talents because the stars and cosmic forces suggest so.

This went on for at least three minutes.

I found it somewhat odd but didn't think too much about it until the next message. It was her again and she went on again in the same fashion for another two minutes. Now I was sure it was odd. I guessed she was trying to reach you and again didn't think much about it. I didn't think it was necessary to reach out to you and say a kooky gal left a message for you on my machine.

I had told a friend about the message, and I was asked if I knew who you were, and I said no. He told me you were a designer for the Gucci family and lived in the neighborhood. I was impressed by that knowledge, and that I was receiving messages for you, no matter how odd they were.

After a week passed, I

received a call from a woman who spoke with an Italian accent who was calling from Italy and asked for Tom Ford. I knew she was looking for you and told her about the two Tom Fords on the upper east side, and she got a good chuckle over it.

She asked if I knew who you were, and I told what I knew and then she spoke so highly of you for at least 10 minutes. She was quite lovely and I suggested she call you before she ran up a large international phone bill talking to *the other* Tom Ford.

I'm hoping she did get in touch with you. The reason for this note at this time is, I am working on a book that reaches back to that timeline and the story came back to me. I'm figuring twenty-some-odd years is a long enough wait and I needed to find a way to share this story of two Tom Fords in

Manhattan's phone book
with you.

Looking forward to my
future in the entertainment
business: it is, without a
doubt, that your suit designs
are my choice when the red
carpet rolls my way.

Thank you for your time and
all the best to you -

Sincerely,
Tom Stratford

As is often the case with the approaching holiday,

life got hectic, and I put my Zita work aside. I had extra

days scheduled at work, festivities to attend, and my

birthday to celebrate. My birthday is mid-December,

smack in the middle of the holiday hoopla and

celebrations, so I have an entire awesome birthday

month, where everyone seems to be celebrating right up

through to the New Year. Even so, I promised myself

that I would get right back to work on Zita right after the turn of the calendar.

New Year's Eve was full of excitement: in addition to all of the festivities at the restaurant, I went out with my friends after work to a neighboring bar, and we welcomed the New Year in with a lot of cheer and laughter. Afterward, I made my way home to relax with a nightcap. I plugged in my Christmas tree, and turned on the *Turner Classic Movie Channel,* which is one of my favorite channels, with the volume off per my usual habit. *The Thin Man* was the classic showing that night. I made myself a Baileys on the rocks and settled in for a purposeful end to the year.

It was time to give Zita my full attention once again. I took out all of my files, notepads, pieces of papers with ideas written on them, and spread everything out on the floor in front of me. It felt good to be surrounded by notebooks and folders filled with pages about Zita. These chronicled an important time and a one-of-a-kind mentor, and just thinking about her filled me with nostalgic memories. As I was enjoying the peace and quiet reflection, my solace was rudely interrupted by a sound that I thought was coming from right behind me, perhaps in the hallway. I looked around but could see nothing out of place or unusual. A few seconds later, another sound - this one of heavy breathing - started to freak me out because it sounded for sure *as if it was coming from somewhere in my apartment. What in the world could be going on? Was I about to be the unwitting and unlucky star in my own Jason-type horror flick?*

I got up from the floor and looked around but could find nothing to explain the sound.

"Ahaha…uhuhuh…mmmhuh.," the sounds continued. I

swept my eyes around my apartment again, and finally realized that the sound was coming from the air conditioner which sat under the dining room window. I walked over to investigate and peered through the blinds as I got to the window. Right beneath my window were two heads, a curly headed guy and a blonde girl, hidden behind the tall shrubs planted there. I couldn't believe my eyes: they were going at it full force; their moans and groans echoing through my air conditioning unit.

I had no idea what to do, and the fact that I had been drinking didn't help. *This threw me for a loop and I was already loopy enough from all of the celebrating!* I paced the room for a few minutes and when I returned to the window, I saw them running across the lawn toward the waist-high metal fencing. The guy jumped right over, but the gal, who was a good bit shorter and who had the misfortune to be wearing a tight and glittering dress, got caught trying to get over. After a moment struggling to get free, next thing I knew, she fell like a rock right onto her backside on the sidewalk below. *Both of her legs were shooting straight up into the air,* giving me more of a view than I had ever wanted, and so I just stood there in my dining room, stunned.

The girl struggled to get up *while the guy just watched.* I wanted to open the window and shout, *"Hey! You just screwed her under my window; the least you can do is to help her get up!"* But I refrained, and I watched as she eventually got back on her feet and they both ran back into the bar where they had likely been partying.

I turned around and surveyed everything which I had laid out on the floor. *Zita, is this my re-introduction to you? You always did have the flair for the dramatic. Was this the way my New Year was going to start?* It looked like I was in for a rough ride ahead, if this was to be the case, and so I decided to make another night cap and call it a night.

Over the next few weeks, my habit of getting to Zita's files was inconsistent. I knew that Ron was waiting for me to send the chapters to him so that he could get them into professional format, but still I slacked off from time-to-time. It wasn't that I lacked motivation, just that my focus sometimes wandered. However, Zita was there to provide me with a few wake-up calls when needed. As I had said earlier in this book, I am someone who believes in the possibility that we can be sent messages from *the great beyond,* and this open outlook on spirituality allowed me to tune into receiving messages from Zita herself.

One of these occurred on one particular night when the *Turner Classic Movie Channel* was paying tribute to the famous Romanian-American actor, Edward G. Robinson. As I walked into the living room from my kitchen, my screen was graced with a close-up scene between Zita and Mr. Robinson. Of course, I stopped and watched it, wondering for a moment if Zita was telling me to get going with her story. I shook it off as mere coincidence and didn't give it too much thought that night, but the very next day, *the exact same scene was playing* as I turned on the set. *What are the odds? This time, I took the occurrence as a very firm kick in the ass right from Zita herself.*

Zita's message, and her calling me back to the time of my devoted loyalty to her, informed me that she needed me once again and was no longer too proud to acknowledge it. Yes, indeed, it was time for me to get moving forward once again with my Zita work, *and I did.* I took a fresh look at my relationship with her and wondered once again how I was going to figure out what happened to *After the End.*

Subsequent to that night, Ron became very busy since he was in such high demand by Hollywood producers. Nonetheless, I had faith that eventually he would get this story onto the radar of an interested party. As Zita had always taught me, *everything happens when things are in the right hands and when it is in its proper time.*

***

Afterword

***

And so, here we go. *Along Came Zita* .... is now a finished book, and there's no telling what may come of it. Perhaps one day, we will find her original manuscript and I can publish it posthumously under her name. Then maybe, I can land the part of Michael in the film version of it, as I had always promised Zita I would.

One thing remains clear and stands out above all other concerns: she and I are both moving forward, *After the End.*

***

Thank you for reading about how my life and Zita's intersected for too brief a moment. I am looking forward to seeing how this journey will go, and it is just now starting.

I recently found this on the website *Findagrave:*

> *Zita Johann: Actress. She is best known for her role as 'Princess Ankhesenamón' in "The Mummy" (1932). She also appeared in "The Struggle" (1931) and "The Sin of Nora Moran" (1933). After another film, she retired, and worked with acting students and young people with learning disorders. She retuned in 1986 in the film "Raiders of the Living Dead", her last movie. She was cremated and her ashes went to the home of a student at Deposit in upstate New York and scattered in a stream on the property there.*

Bio by: <u>José L Bernabé Tronchoni</u>[2]

Under the title "Family Members," it listed only one name and photo, that of John Houseman. As of this writing, 348 people left flowers for Zita on this webpage. Although I read them all, I did not recognize any of the well-wishers' names or see anybody famous. Plenty of them were her adoring fans who mentioned what a great impact Zita's role in *The Mummy* had left on them.

By the way, you can leave a flower and comment for Zita by typing or pasting the web address just below into your browser:

https://www.findagrave.com/memorial/6983891/zita-johann/flower

[1] Tronchoni, José L Bernabé. *Memorial for Zita Johann.* Findagrave: updated August 30, 2022. Accessed November 23, 2022. https://www.findagrave.com/memorial/6983891/zita-johann

***

Thanks to-

The wonderful Desiree & Eric Maikranz

Maura Zugibe and the memory of Kevin Zugibe.

Jim Shooter & Debbie Fix for relighting the fire.

Bonnie Timm for constant support.

LuAnn Weis and David Cenicola putting things together.

Joe & Rita Stratford for everything.

Zita Johann and all of her wonderful fans out there.

***

Table of Authorities:

Grimes, William. *Zita Johann Dead; Actress, 89, Played The Mummy's Love.* New York Times, Sept. 30, 1993. Accessed November 23, 2022. https://www.nytimes.com/1993/09/30/obituaries/zita-johann-dead-actress-89-played-the-mummy-s-love.html

Tronchoni, José L Bernabé. *Memorial for Zita Johann.* Findagrave: updated August 30, 2022. Accessed November 23, 2022. https://www.findagrave.com/memorial/6983891/zita-johann